ANSWERS TO LIFE'S
MOST PERPLEXING
PROBLEMS

Ten Christian Leaders Share Their Insights

Multnomah Books *Sisters, Oregon*

TEN ANSWERS TO LIFE'S MOST PERPLEXING PROBLEMS
published by Multnomah Publishers, Inc.

©1998 by Multnomah Publishers, Inc.
International Standard Book Number: 1-57673-302-5

Scripture quotations are from:
The Holy Bible, New International Version (NIV) © 1973, 1984 by
International Bible Society, used by permission of
Zondervan Publishing House.

New American Standard Bible (NASB) © 1960, 1977 by the Lockman Foundation

The Living Bible (LB) © 1971. Used by permission of Tyndale House Publishers, Inc.

The Holy Bible, New King James Version (NKJV) © 1984 by Thomas Nelson, Inc.

The Holy Bible, King James Version (KJV)

Printed in the United States of America

For information:
MULTNOMAH PUBLISHERS, INC.•POST OFFICE BOX 1720•SISTERS, OREGON 97759

98 99 00 01 02 03 04 — 10 9 8 7 6 5 4 3 2 1

CONTENTS

PREFACE

The problems in this book are real—nearly everyone deals with them at some time in his or her life. You can choose to

- Ignore the problems—they usually get worse.
- Try to solve them on your own—they usually get more complicated.
- Seek help from biblical specialists—the problems usually get resolved.

The contributors to the book *are* biblical specialists. They not only have experience in their fields, but they tap into the issues from a biblical perspective. Here at your fingertips, you have counsel from the best.

Each of the selections provides valuable information. The chapters on parenting and money may make you squirm a bit. The information on death and values yields life principles worth adopting. The release you'll receive from the chapters on guilt and bitterness, morality, forgiveness, depression, and self-image can be life saving. The chapter on marriage alone is worth the price of the book.

So you can start at the beginning and find answers to life's struggles, or pick and choose the subjects you are struggling with.

Remember, it's not wrong to have problems, but it's potentially devastating to be passive about them.

A Struggling Traveler
John Van Diest
General Editor

Struggling with Guilt and Bitterness

MAX LUCADO

Max Lucado
Pastor, speaker on national radio program "UpWords"
Popular author of many award-winning books

Guilt

Rebecca Thompson fell twice from the Fremont Canyon Bridge. She died both times. The first fall broke her heart; the second broke her neck.

She was only eighteen years of age when she and her eleven-year-old sister were abducted by a pair of hoodlums near a store in Casper, Wyoming. They drove the girls forty miles southwest to the Fremont Canyon Bridge, a one-lane, steelbeamed structure rising 112 feet above the North Platte River.

The men brutally beat and raped Rebecca. She somehow convinced them not to do the same to her sister Amy. Both were thrown over the bridge into the narrow gorge. Amy died when she landed on a rock near the river, but Rebecca slammed into a ledge and was ricocheted into deeper water.

With a hip fractured in five places, she struggled to the shore. To protect her body from the cold, she wedged herself between two rocks and waited until the dawn.

But the dawn never came to Rebecca. Oh, the sun came up, and she was found. The physicians treated her wounds, and the

9

courts imprisoned her attackers. Life continued, but the dawn never came.

The blackness of her night of horrors lingered. She was never able to climb out of the canyon. So in September 1992, nineteen years later, she returned to the bridge.

Against her boyfriend's pleadings, she drove seventy miles-per-hour to the North Platte River. With her two-year-old daughter and boyfriend at her side, she sat on the edge of the Fremont Canyon Bridge and wept. Through her tears she retold the story. The boyfriend didn't want the child to see her mother cry, so he carried the toddler to the car.

That's when he heard her body hit the water.

And that's when Rebecca Thompson died her second death. The sun never dawned on Rebecca's dark night. Why? What eclipsed the light from her world?

Fear? Perhaps. She had testified against the men, pointing them out in the courtroom. One of the murderers had taunted her by smirking and sliding his finger across his throat. On the day of her death, the two had been up for parole. Perhaps the fear of a second encounter was too great.

Was it anger? Anger at her rapists? Anger at the parole board? Anger at herself for the thousand falls in the thousand nightmares that followed? Or anger at God for a canyon that grew ever deeper and a night that grew ever blacker and a dawn that never came?

Was it guilt? Some think so. Despite Rebecca's attractive smile and appealing personality, friends say that she struggled with the ugly fact that she had survived and her little sister had not.

Was it shame? Everyone she knew and thousands she didn't had heard the humiliating details of her tragedy. The stigma was tattooed deeper with the newspaper ink of every headline. She had been raped. She had been violated. She had been shamed. And try as she might to outlive and outrun the memory…she never could.

So nineteen years later she went back to the bridge.

Canyons of shame run deep. Gorges of never-ending guilt. Walls ribboned with the greens and grays of death. Unending echoes of screams. Put your hands over your ears. Splash water on your face. Stop looking over your shoulder. Try as you might to outrun yesterday's tragedies—their tentacles are longer than your hope. They draw you back to the bridge of sorrows to be shamed again and again and again.

If it was your fault, it would be different. If you were to blame, you could apologize. If the tumble into the canyon was your mistake, you could respond. But you weren't a volunteer. You were a victim.

Sometimes your shame is private. Pushed over the edge by an abusive spouse. Molested by a perverted parent. Seduced by a compromising superior. No one else knows. But you know. And that's enough.

Sometimes it's public. Branded by a divorce you didn't want. Contaminated by a disease you never expected. Marked by a handicap you didn't create. And whether it's actually in their eyes or just in your imagination, you have to deal with it—you are marked: a divorcee, an invalid, an orphan, an AIDS patient.

Whether private or public, shame is always painful. And unless you deal with it, it is permanent. Unless you get help—the dawn will never come.

You're not surprised when I say there are Rebecca Thompsons in every city and Fremont Bridges in every town. And there are many Rebecca Thompsons in the Bible. So many, in fact, that it almost seems that the pages of Scripture are stitched together with their stories. You've met many in this book. Each acquainted with the hard floor of the canyon of shame.

But there is one woman whose story embodies them all. A story of failure. A story of abuse. A story of shame. And a story of grace.

That's her, the woman standing in the center of the circle. Those men around her are religious leaders. Pharisees, they are called. Self-appointed custodians of conduct. And the other man, the one in the simple clothes, the one sitting on the ground, the one looking at the face of the woman, that's Jesus.

Jesus has been teaching.

The woman has been cheating.

And the Pharisees are out to stop them both.

"Teacher, this woman was caught in the act of adultery" (John 8:4, NIV). The accusation rings off the courtyard walls.

"Caught." Aha! What have we here? This man is not your husband. Put on some clothes! We know what to do with women like you!

In an instant she is yanked from private passion to public spectacle. Heads poke out of windows as the posse pushes her through the streets. Dogs bark. Neighbors turn. The city sees. Clutching a thin robe around her shoulders, she hides her nakedness.

But nothing can hide her shame.

From this second on, she'll be known as an adulteress. When she goes to the market, women will whisper. When she passes, heads will turn. When her name is mentioned, the people will remember.

Moral failure finds easy recall.

The greater travesty, however, goes unnoticed. What the woman did is shameful, but what the Pharisees did is despicable. According to the law, adultery was punishable by death, but only if two people witnessed the act. There had to be two eyewitnesses.

Question: How likely are two people to be eyewitnesses to adultery? What are the chances of two people stumbling upon an early morning flurry of forbidden embraces? Unlikely. But if you do, odds are it's not a coincidence.

So we wonder. How long did the men peer through the window before they barged in? How long did they lurk behind the curtain before they stepped out?

And what of the man? Adultery requires two participants. What happened to him? Could it be that he slipped out?

The evidence leaves little doubt. It was a trap. She's been caught. But she'll soon see that she is not the catch—she's only the bait.

"The law of Moses commands that we stone to death every woman who does this. What do you say we should do?" (John 8:5).

Pretty cocky, this committee of high ethics. Pretty proud of themselves, these agents of righteousness. This will be a moment they long remember, the morning they foil and snag the mighty Nazarene.

As for the woman? Why, she's immaterial. Merely a pawn in their game. Her future? It's unimportant. Her reputation? Who cares if it's ruined? She is a necessary, yet dispensable, part of their plan.

The woman stares at the ground. Her sweaty hair dangles. Her tears drip hot with hurt. Her lips are tight, her jaw is clenched. She knows she's been framed. No need to look up. She'll find no kindness. She looks at the stones in their hands. Squeezed so tightly that fingertips turn white.

She thinks of running. But where? She could claim mistreatment. But to whom? She could deny the act, but she was seen. She could beg for mercy, but these men offer none.

The woman has nowhere to turn.

You'd expect Jesus to stand and proclaim judgment on the hypocrites. He doesn't. You'd hope that he would snatch the woman and the two would be beamed to Galilee. That's not what happens either. You'd imagine that an angel would descend or heaven would speak or the earth would shake. No, none of that.

Once again, his move is subtle.

But, once again, his message is unmistakable.

What does Jesus do? (If you already know, pretend you don't and feel the surprise.)

Jesus writes in the sand.

He stoops down and draws in the dirt. The same finger that

engraved the commandments on Sinai's peak and seared the warning on Belshazzar's wall now scribbles in the courtyard floor. And as he write, he speaks: "Anyone here who has never sinned can throw the first stone at her" (John 8:7).

The young look to the old. The old look in their hearts. They are the first to drop their stones. And as they turn to leave, the young who were cocky with borrowed convictions do the same. The only sound is the thud of rocks and the shuffle of feet.

Jesus and the woman are left alone. With the jury gone, the courtroom becomes the judge's chambers, and the woman awaits his verdict. *Surely, a sermon is brewing. No doubt, he's going to demand that I apologize.* But the judge doesn't speak. His head is down, perhaps he's still writing in the sand. He seems surprised when he realizes that she is still there.

"Woman, where are they? Has no one judged you guilty?"

She answers, "No one, sir."

Then Jesus says, "I also don't judge you guilty. You may go now, but don't sin anymore" (John 8:10–11).

If you have ever wondered how God reacts when you fail, frame these words and hang them on the wall. Read them. Ponder them. Drink from them. Stand below them and let them wash over your soul.

And then listen. Listen carefully. He's speaking.

"I don't judge you guilty."

And watch. Watch carefully. He's writing. He's leaving a message. Not in the sand, but on a cross.

Not with his hand, but with his blood.

His message has two words: Not guilty.

The Dungeon of Bitterness

The case of the elder brother.

A difficult one because he looked so good. He kept his room straight and his nose clean. He played by the rules and paid all his dues. His résumé? Impeccable. His credit? Squeaky clean. And loyalty? While his brother was sowing wild oats, he stayed home and sowed the crops.

On the outside he was everything a father could want in a son. But on the inside he was sour and hollow. Overcome by jealousy. Consumed by anger. Blinded by bitterness.

You remember the story. It's perhaps the best known of all the parables Jesus told. It's the third of three stories in Luke 15, three stories of three parties.

The first began after a shepherd found a sheep he'd lost. He had ninety-nine others. He could have been content to write this one off as a loss. But shepherds don't think like businessmen. So he searched for it. When he found the sheep, he carried it back to the flock, cut the best grass for the sheep to eat, and had a party to celebrate.

The second party was held in front of a house. A housewife had lost a coin. It wasn't her only coin, but you would have thought it was by the way she acted. She moved the furniture, got out the dust mop, and swept the whole house till she found it. And when she did, she ran shouting into the cul-de-sac and invited her neighbors over for a party to celebrate.

Then there is the story of the lost son. The boy who broke his father's heart by taking his inheritance and taking off. He trades his dignity for a whisky bottle and his self-respect for a pigpen. Then comes the son's sorrow and his decision to go home. He hopes his dad will give him a job on the farm and an apartment over the garage. What he finds is a father who has kept his absent son's place set at the table and the porch light on every night.

The father is so excited so see his son, you'll never guess what he does. That's right! He throws a party! We party-loving prodigals love what he did, but it infuriated the elder brother.

"The older son was angry" (Luke 15:28). It's not hard to see why. "So, is this how a guy gets recognition in this family? Get drunk and go broke and you get a party?" So he sat outside the house and pouted.

I did that once. I pouted at a party. A Christmas party. I was in the fourth grade. Fourth graders take parties very seriously, especially when there are gifts involved. We had drawn names. Since you didn't know who had your name, you had to drop your hints very loudly. I didn't miss a chance. I wanted a "Sixth Finger"—a toy pistol that fit in the cleft of your hand and looked like a finger. (Honestly, it did exist!)

Finally the day came to open the gifts. I just knew I was going to get my pistol. Everyone in the class had heard my hints. I tore into the wrapping and ripped open the box and…know what I got? Stationery. Western stationery. Paper and envelopes with horses in the corners. Yuck! Probably left over from the Christmas before. Ten-year-old boys don't write letters! What was this person thinking? No doubt some mom forgot all about the present until this morning, so she went to the closet and rumbled about until she came out with stationery.

Tie my hands and feet and throw me in the river. I was distraught. I was upset. So I missed the party. I was present, but I pouted.

So did the big brother. He, too, felt he was a victim of inequity. When his father came out to meet him, the son started at the top, listing the atrocities of his life. To hear him say it, his woes began the day he was born.

"I have served you like a slave for many years and have always obeyed your commands. But you never gave me even a young goat to have at a feast with my friends. But your other son, who wasted all your money on prostitutes, comes home, and you kill the fat calf for him!" (Luke 15:29–30).

Appears that both sons spent time in the pigpen. One in the pen of rebellion—the other in the pen of self-pity. The younger one has come home. The older one hasn't. He's still in the slop. He is saying the same thing you said when the kid down the street got a bicycle and you didn't. It's not fair!

That's what Wanda Holloway of Channelview, Texas, said.

When it looked like her fourteen-year-old daughter wouldn't get elected to the cheerleading squad, Wanda got angry. She decided to get even. She hired a hit man to kill the mother of her daughter's chief competitor, hoping to so upset the girl that Wanda's daughter would make the squad. Bitterness will do that to you. It'll cause you to burn down your house to kill a rat.

Fortunately, her plan failed and Wanda Holloway was caught. She was sentenced to fifteen years. She didn't have to be put behind bars to be imprisoned, however. Bitterness is its own prison.

Black and cold, bitterness denies easy escape. The sides are slippery with resentment. A floor of muddy anger stills the feet. The stench of betrayal fills the air and stings the eyes. A cloud of self-pity blocks the view of the tiny exit above.

Step in and look at the prisoners. Victims are chained to the walls. Victims of betrayal. Victims of abuse. Victims of the government, the system, the military, the world. They lift their chains as they lift their voices and wail.

Loud and long they wail.

They grumble. They're angry at others who got what they didn't.

They sulk. The world is against them.

They accuse. The pictures of their enemies are darted to the wall.

They boast. "I followed the rules. I played fairly...in fact, better than anybody else."

They whine. "Nobody listens to me. Nobody remembers me. Nobody cares about me."

Angry. Sullen. Accusatory. Arrogant. Whiny. Put them all together in one word and spell it b-i-t-t-e-r. If you put them all in one person, that person is in the pit—the dungeon of bitterness.

The dungeon, deep and dark, is beckoning you to enter.

You can, you know. You've experienced enough hurt. You've been betrayed enough times. You have a history of rejections, don't you? Haven't you been left out, left behind, or left out in the cold? You are a candidate for the dungeon.

You can choose, like many, to chain yourself to your hurt.

Or you can choose, like some, to put away your hurts before they become hates. You can choose to go to the party. You have a place there. Your name is beside a plate. If you are a child of God, no one can take away your sonship.

Which is precisely what the father said to the older son. "Son, you are always with me, and all that I have is yours" (Luke 15:31).

And that is precisely what the Father says to you. How does God deal with your bitter heart? He reminds you that what you have is more important than what you don't have. You still have your relationship with God. No one can take that. No one can touch it.

Your health can be taken and your money stolen—but your place at God's table is permanent.

The brother was bitter because he focused on what he didn't have and forgot what he did have. His father reminded him—and us—that he had everything he'd always had. He had his job. His place. His name. His inheritance. The only thing he didn't have was the spotlight. And because he wasn't content to share it—he missed the party.

It takes courage to set aside jealousy and rejoice with the achievements of a rival. Would you like an example of someone who did?

Standing before ten thousand eyes is Abraham Lincoln. An uncomfortable Abraham Lincoln. His discomfort comes not from the thought of delivering his first inaugural address but from the ambitious efforts of well-meaning tailors. He's unaccustomed to such attire—formal black dress coat, silk vest, black trousers, and a glossy top hat. He holds a huge ebony cane with a golden head the size of an egg.

He approaches the platform with hat in one hand and cane in the other. He doesn't know what to do with either one. In the nervous silence that comes after the applause and before the speech, he searches for a spot to place them. He finally leans the cane in a corner of the railing, but he still doesn't know what to do with the hat. He could lay it on the podium, but it would take up too much room. Perhaps the floor...no, too dirty.

Just then, and not a moment too soon, a man steps forward and takes the hat, returns to his seat, and listens intently to Lincoln's speech.

Who is he? Lincoln's dearest friend. The president said of him, "He and I are about the best friends in the world."

He was one of the strongest supporters of the early stages of Lincoln's presidency. He was given the honor of escorting Mrs. Lincoln in the inaugural grand ball. As the storm of the Civil War began to boil, many of Lincoln's friends left, but not this one. He amplified his loyalty by touring the South as Lincoln's peace ambassador. He begged Southerners not to secede and Northerners to rally behind the president.

His efforts were great, but the wave of anger was greater. The country did divide, and civil war bloodied the nation. Lincoln's friend never lived to see it. He died three months after Lincoln's inauguration. Wearied by his travels, he succumbed to a fever, and Lincoln was left to face the war alone.

Upon hearing the news of his friend's death, Lincoln wept openly and ordered the White House flag to be flown at half-staff. Some feel Lincoln's friend would have been chosen as his running mate in 1864 and would thus have become president following the assassination of the Great Emancipator.

No one will ever know about that. But we do know that Lincoln had one true friend. And we can only imagine the number of times the memory of him brought warmth to a cold Oval Office. He was a model of friendship.

He was also a model of forgiveness.

This friend could just as easily have been an enemy. Long before he and Lincoln were allies, they were competitors—politicians pursuing the same office. And unfortunately, their debates are better known than their friendship. The debates between Abraham Lincoln and his dear friend, Stephen A. Douglas.

But on Lincoln's finest day, Douglas set aside their differences and held the hat of the president. Unlike the older brother, Douglas heard a higher call. And unlike the older brother, he was present at the party.

Wise are we if we do the same. Wise are we if we rise above our hurts. For if we do, we'll be present at the Father's final celebration. A party to end all parties. A party where no pouters will be permitted.

Why don't you come and join the fun?

Struggling

with Forgiveness

LUIS PALAU

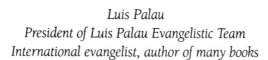

Luis Palau
President of Luis Palau Evangelistic Team
International evangelist, author of many books

Billy Staton slipped a recording device into his shirt before going to pick up his daughter for a picnic, planning to tape his ex-wife's hostility about his visitation rights.

Instead, Staton recorded his own slaying in what one prosecutor called "twenty-three minutes of murder." Paul Wolf, twenty-one, was charged with Staton's death. According to the state prosecutors, the tape conclusively proved that Wolf committed the brutal murder. But the Associated Press reported that he pleaded *innocent* to the slaying.

Wolf's attorney told the jurors that his client was innocent because he was "legally insane" the day of the killing. He explained that Wolf had had a difficult childhood, then faced an ongoing series of custody problems after his marriage to Staton's ex-wife.

The attorney explained that Wolf did not plan the killing, but was *forced* to bludgeon twenty-six-year-old Staton to death "at the last minute after the steady, lengthy, continual buildup of the pressure."

Are you surprised when you read of our court records being

filled day after day with excuses for criminal actions? Probably not. It's almost expected these days. Admitting one's guilt has become passé. Instead, our society works doubletime trying to cover up personal responsibility with carefully constructed explanations for wrong-doing.

Tell me, whatever happened to *sin*?

In the April 4, 1983, *Newsweek*, psychologist Rex Julien Beaber pointed out:

> The new 'sciences' of sociology, psychology and psychiatry have cast aside such concepts as will, will power, badness and laziness and replaced them with political and psychological repression, poor conditioning, diseased family interaction and bad genes. One by one, human failings have been redesignated as diseases.

Beaber counters this modern trend by stating: "The American lust for scientific-sounding explanations is completely out of control.... Ultimately, we must assume responsibility for our actions."

Sin needs to be rediscovered once more in our generation.

RECOGNIZING OUR NEED FOR GOD'S FORGIVENESS

Isn't it strange that even as Christians we blush to hear a fellow Christian speak of "sin" or "guilt" outside the four walls of a church? If the truth were known, I suspect that many believers have scratched both words out of their working vocabulary. In doing so, they have made "forgiveness" absolutely meaningless.

But as we turn to the compass of our Christian experience, the Bible, we find its pages providing much needed reality therapy. It is no coincidence that only four chapters within all of Scripture—the first two and the last two—remain silent about sin, its consequences, and its remedy. Since Adam and Eve found themselves standing naked under the Tree of Knowledge of Good and Evil, sin has been the lowest common denominator throughout the human race.

The apostle John spells this out clearly: "If we claim to be without sin, we deceive ourselves and the truth is not in us" (1 John 1:8, NIV). The deadliest sin is assuming we have none. No one is free from the possibility of committing evil. Until we enjoy fruit from the Tree of Life in glory some day, we must admit our vulnerability.

Listen to what William Wilberforce, nineteenth century British politician and reformer, says in his book *Real Christianity*: "There is no shortcut to holiness. It must be the business of [our] whole lives." We can't be holy in a hurry.

One evening a number of years ago I was rushing around the house trying to get ready for a trip—and becoming more frustrated every minute. The boys still weren't in bed, my suitcases weren't packed, and it was getting late! It was my own fault, but the whole family had to suffer with me.

When I finally went to my bedroom that night, I found a note on my pillow. This is what it said:

Dad is mad.

I am sad.

I'm not glad 'cause Dad is mad,

So, Lord, change Dad.

It was signed by all four of my boys. I'll tell you that humbled me. I laughed. I shed a tear. I went to every bed and hugged my boys and kissed them and asked for their forgiveness.

As a father, I know I must admit my own shortcomings to my children if I am to earn their respect. I can't pretend that I don't sin, or am somehow immune to certain temptations.

COLLAPSE IN THE CHRISTIAN LIFE

"If you're saying some sin could never get you," Dr. Howard Hendricks says, "you're about to step on a spiritual banana peel."

Assuming invincibility is never a fail-safe security.

You and I both know of Christian leaders and laymen who have "suddenly" fallen into sin. Everything seems to be going well for them, then they leave their spouse for someone else...they attempt suicide...they become alcoholic.

Within the last two years I have learned of several well-known leaders who have fallen into serious sin. I have known one of these men for years. He was an outgoing, winsome fellow who preached strongly against sin.

Then one day he left his family and took up with another woman. He admits making some mistakes, but he blames his wife, he blames the Lord, he blames his friends—everybody but himself.

How does something like this happen? Dr. George Sweeting comments, "Collapse in the Christian life is rarely a blowout—it's usually a slow leak." In the particular case I mentioned above, this Christian leader had been secretly filling his mind with pornography for years. Once he allowed his focus to shift from the things of the Lord, the world quickly offered him a subtle but destructive "thrill" as a substitute.

Our spiritual life is punctured and in danger of collapse whenever we lose sight of who God is. To the degree that we do not know God, we sin. Sin becomes our declaration of independence from His sovereignty.

Our acts of independence—whether in deed, thought, or desire—produce certain results. When we sin the Holy Spirit is grieved, Satan gains a foothold, we lose our joy in Christ, we feel ourselves separated from God and others, we become a stumbling block to weaker brothers, and we cause untold sorrow and grief.

Take spiritual inventory of your own life. Consider:

- *Who is God in my eyes?*
- *What is my relationship with Him like?*
- *Have I tried to assert my independence?*
- *Is there unresolved guilt in my life?*

Is the Lord speaking to your heart? Don't ignore what He's saying! Instead of burying our guilt feelings—pretending they don't exist—we need to seek, to know, and to experience God's forgiveness.

LETTING GO OF GUILT

Sometimes what we consider to be guilt is nothing more than feelings aroused by false condemnation. When I was a teenager, my mother absolutely believed the bottom of the theater would open up and drop me straight into the fire of hell if I ever went to see a movie, regardless of its message. I felt bad even to walk past a theater. Now *that* was false guilt.

Paul Tournier, a respected Swiss psychologist, has accurately observed, "False guilt comes as a result of judgments and suggestions of men." People sometimes seek to control or manipulate us by inventing rules or regulations about issues the Bible never addresses. We need to carefully and prayerfully identify such false guilt and let go of it.

On other occasions we carry a heavy burden of guilt because we have never dealt with it properly. Throughout my years of ministry I have seen at least three inadequate responses to true guilt.

Inadequate Response #1: We can *repress* our guilt. We try to cover it up and deny its existence. Or we focus on our insignificant faults instead of acknowledging our real guilt. As a result, we lose our inner peace and even suffer physically, sometimes unconscious of what we are doing to ourselves.

Each year my Team and I receive thousands of letters in response to our crusades and television and radio broadcasts. One day we received a letter from a woman who wrote:

I often feel spiritually and physically weak. I'm almost enslaved by my nerves. At times, everything irritates me. It's not because my marriage is bad. During our four years of marriage we've never had any problems or anything to threaten our happiness. I don't want to go to a doctor because I've lost confidence in them. But what can I do?

On the outside, this woman said life seemed to be going her way. But on the inside she was going to pieces. In my response to her, I pointed out that our emotions don't bother us without reason. They respond when something isn't going right in our lives physically, emotionally, or spiritually. So I made the following recommendations.

In the first place, I told this woman not to disregard the help of a good medical doctor. Her problem could have an organic origin. She needed to see a doctor, even if she had lost confidence in them. I warned her, however, not just to ask for tranquilizers to mask her condition. By asking for a thorough physical examination, she could find out if the source of her nervous problems was at least partially physical.

On the other hand, I encouraged her to be honest with herself. "Are you bitter against someone?" I asked. "Is there unresolved guilt in your life? Are you worrying? Don't repress these things. They will only trouble your nerves more." Repression can produce the same symptoms she described in her letter. It can have devastating effects in our lives.

Inadequate Response #2: We can *regret* our "mistakes." But when we say, "I'm sorry," and seek to justify our actions, we fail to acknowledge the seriousness of our sin and our responsibility. Corrie ten Boom once said, "The blood of Jesus never cleansed an excuse."

While perusing a special feature on youth in an issue of the London *Daily Mail*, I read an interview featuring an eighteen-year-old-girl named Sarah. Notice what she says:

If I had my time over again, I wouldn't have gotten married so soon. Not many of my friends are married with babies already—and I feel very envious of them sometimes. One girl I know has a Porsche, and what have I got? A baby and this cramped little flat and no money....

Andy and I met at school and we got married when I was 16 because I was pregnant. I'll never forget the panic. Andy was in Cyprus and I was living at home with my Dad and I didn't dare tell him. My parents separated when I was 11 and I just didn't know where to turn.

Sarah went on to say:

I hope Andy and I will stay together, though being a soldier he's away a lot, and I get bored being stuck at home all day, so maybe one day we'll split up. The thing is you have to try so hard to make marriage work and divorce is so easy.

Like so many others, Sarah regretted the *consequences* of her actions, but that's all. She expressed no sense of having done wrong by being involved in premarital sex.

Inadequate Response #3: We can feel *remorse* for our sin. "I wish I'd never done that," we say and promise we'll never do it again. And we're completely sincere. We really do feel bad about what we've done.

Remorse is "a gnawing distress arising from a sense of guilt for past actions," according to the dictionary. And it will eat you alive. Ask Judas.

Early in the morning, all the chief priests and elders of the people came to the decision to put Jesus to death. They bound him, led him away, and handed him over to Pilate, the governor.

When Judas, who had betrayed him, saw that Jesus was condemned, he was seized with remorse and returned the thirty silver coins to the chief priests and the elders. "I have sinned," he said, "for I have betrayed innocent blood."

"What is that to us?" they replied. "That's your responsibility" (Matthew 27:1–4, NIV).

Remorse seized Judas once more, ripping his soul with convulsions. The highest religious leaders of the land had just slammed the door on what seemed to be his only hope for atonement. So Judas threw the money into the temple and left. Then he went away and hanged himself (Matthew 27:5).

Judas knew the seriousness of his crime. He admitted he had condemned the sinless Son of Man. But he fell one step short of what the Bible calls "repentance."

THE CORRECT RESPONSE

Repentance is the biblical, correct response to sin. The moment we committed our life to Christ, our sins—past, present, and future—were forgiven. God's righteousness was satisfied. But now as children of God we must maintain fellowship by confessing our sins to our heavenly Father as we become aware of them.

C. S. Lewis said that true guilt is an inner alarm system which reveals sin in our lives and shows our loss of fellowship with God. The Holy Spirit uses guilt to prompt us to turn *from* our sin and back *to* the Father.

Once we let go of false guilt and properly deal with our sins, we are free to revel in God's mercy. Proverbs 28:13 explains, "He who conceals his sins does not prosper, but whoever confesses and renounces them finds mercy."

Isaiah 55:6–7 adds this assurance: "Seek the LORD while he may be found; call on him while he is near. Let the wicked forsake his way and the evil man his thoughts. Let him turn to the LORD, and he will have mercy on him, and to our God, for he will freely pardon."

While we don't deserve God's mercy, of course, He offers us complete pardon anyway.

A mother once approached Napoleon seeking a pardon for her son. The emperor replied that the young man committed a certain offense twice, and justice demanded death.

"But I don't ask for justice," the mother explained. "I plead for mercy."

"But your son does not deserve mercy," Napoleon replied.

"Sir," the woman cried, "It would not be mercy if he deserved it, and mercy is all I ask for."

"Well, then," the emperor said, "I will have mercy." And he spared the woman's son.

The beauty of Scripture is its good news that God freely and willingly bestows mercy on anyone who properly confesses his sins. We needn't fear finding God in an unforgiving mood.

Manasseh was one of the most wicked men to serve as king of Judah. He overturned Hezekiah's reforms and served false gods with more zeal than the nations God had originally destroyed before the Israelites (2 Chronicles 33:1–9). But after being captured by the Assyrians, Manasseh greatly humbled himself before the Lord—and God forgave him! (2 Chronicles 33:11–13).

If God forgave such a wicked and pagan king as Manasseh, who humbled himself before the Lord, surely he will have mercy on us when we truly confess our sins and repent. The apostle James tells us, "Humble yourselves before the Lord, and he will lift you up" (James 4:10, NIV). Elsewhere, God goes on to promise, "'Their sins and lawless acts I will remember no more'" (Hebrews 10:17).

How remarkable it is that the omniscient Lord of the universe promises not only to forgive our sins, but also to forget them forever! Whenever I think of that promise in Hebrews 10:17, I can't help recalling how God used it in a special way to transform a hardened Marxist-Leninist into a beautiful child of God.

Would God Forgive Me?

A woman whom I later learned was the secretary of the Communist Party in Ecuador, called me one day and asked for an interview at 9:30 the next morning. Rather, I *thought* we were going to have an interview.

After arriving promptly at 9:30 A.M. and carefully checking my office for hidden recording devices, this woman launched into the most vicious tirade I have ever heard. For more than twenty minutes she berated everything that stood for Christ that she could think of, including me. Bitterness gushed from her and left me speechless.

When she stopped to catch her breath I asked, "Madam, what is your name?"

"Why do you want to know?" she demanded.

I replied, "Well, you've said a lot of things here and I don't even know you." After some thought she announced that she was Maria Benitez-Perez. And then for the next three hours, without a pause or interruption, she told me her violent, pathetic life story. It sounded like the plot of a grade-B movie, reeking with sin and guilt.

Finally she paused and then asked, "Palau, supposing there is a God, would He accept a woman like me?"

"Look, Maria," I replied, "don't worry about what I think; look at what God says." I opened to Hebrews 10:17 and turned the Bible so she could see.

"But I don't believe in the Bible—"

"But we're just supposing there's a God, right?" I interjected. "Let's just suppose the Bible is His Word. He says, 'Their sins and lawless acts I will remember no more.'"

She waited, as if there had to be more. I said nothing. "But listen, I've been an adulteress, married three times, and in bed with a lot of different men."

I said, "'Their sins and lawless acts I will remember no more.'" And began counting the times I repeated that verse.

Seventeen times I responded to Maria's objections and confessions with that verse. It was past lunchtime. I was tired and weak. I had no more to offer. "Would you like Christ to forgive all that you've told me about and all the rest I don't even know?"

She was quiet. Finally she spoke softly. "If He could forgive

me and change me, it would be the greatest miracle in the world."
Within ten minutes I witnessed that miracle as she confessed her
sins, asked for forgiveness, and received Christ.

Today Maria is actively serving the Lord and is an amazing
testimony to the redemptive work of Christ; God wants all of us
to repent of our sins and experience His complete forgiveness.
And not just at the moment of salvation, but on a daily basis.

CONFESSING OUR SINS TO OTHERS

Even after God forgives our sins and forgets them forever, our past
isn't magically erased. Hurt and angry people still lie along the
way behind us. With God's help we must go back to each one we
can find and ask for their forgiveness.

Do you remember the story of Joseph? He's one of my favorite
Bible characters, and you can read about him in Genesis 37–50.
Scripture tells us that when Joseph was just a teenager his broth-
ers sold him into slavery and faked his death.

Did Joseph's brothers go scot-free for what they did? Hardly.
On the contrary, they carried a debilitating burden of guilt with
them wherever they went. Each time they found themselves in a
predicament they said, "'Surely we are being punished because of
our brother'" (Genesis 42:21, NIV). For twenty long years they
were haunted by a skeleton they kept locked away.

If you scratch the surface, most people are desperately trying
to hide a skeleton in some closet, hoping no one will ever find
them out. At the advice of their psychiatrist, they deny their
immorality. They explain away their abusive behavior. They
repress their bitterness. They do anything but admit their sins.
Ironically, until they make such an admission their closet full of
guilt will continue to haunt them.

What skeletons are you hiding in your closet?

You can point your finger and make excuses, you can invent
arguments and do anything else you want, but the key to the
closet jingles in your pocket until you settle matters right.

How long have you kept that skeleton locked in some closet of your soul? Oh, you hope no one ever probes there. You hope no one ever finds a key and says, "Ah! There it is!"

I beg you to take that skeleton out of your closet. Confess your sins to God and to whomever you have offended. Get rid of it and experience God's merciful forgiveness today.

Certain things may never be quite the same, but you can start walking with God again. With total freedom and complete joy you will be able to look every man and woman in the eye as you continue your earthly pilgrimage. Why? Because you're forgiven. Clean. At peace with God and others.

The Bible says, "Confess your sins to each other and pray for each other so that you may be healed" (James 5:16, NIV). Confession is the healing balm of our soul. Our confessions, however, need only be as public as the sin.

I want to suggest a project that will help you settle the things of the past. Go to the Lord today and say, "Lord, here is a piece of paper and a pen. Whatever you bring to mind that you think I should clear up, I will write down."

This sounds easy at first, but it's not. Yet it is rougher to carry sin with you than to confess it and experience release. Why? Because your burdens collect interest, and they get heavier with each new day. Imagine carrying a horrible weight around your neck for the next fifty years. It is not worth it, my friend. Clear it up and you will be at peace.

After you have made your list, lay it down before the Lord. (No one else needs to see it, so destroy it as soon as you can.) Confess your sins to Him. Then determine how you will contact each person on your list to ask for his forgiveness and make restitution, if necessary.

Restitution is often the forgotten factor in forgiveness, but the Bible clearly teaches we must pay back anything we have damaged or stolen (see Exodus 22:1–15).

The question sometimes arises, "Why can't I put my finger on the sins God is pointing out in my heart? I just feel a vague uneasiness." I don't believe the Holy Spirit leaves us guessing when He reveals sin in our lives. Satan, on the other hand, is the master of causing us to feel a generalized sense of guilt and unworthiness. When his cloud of gloom hangs over our head, we should submit ourselves to God and resist the devil (James 4:7).

God doesn't want us to go around introspectively engaged in self-analysis. Instead, He does want us to be sensitive to His Spirit when He points out specific sins, no matter how small or insignificant they may seem to us. Often our offenses don't seem so little to those we've hurt.

FORGIVING OTHERS

But what do we do when others wrong us? What do we do when someone says something destructive about us? When someone takes advantage of us financially? When someone walks out of our life? Again, the story of Joseph is instructive.

The Bible gives us many reasons why Joseph could have been a very bitter man. Not only had his brothers hated him and sold him into slavery, but his master's wife falsely accused him of a serious crime and had him thrown into an Egyptian prison. Later, a government official promised to try to secure his release but left him there to rot. Despite all these things, Joseph did not allow any root of bitterness to take hold in his life (see Hebrews 12:15). Unfortunately, that can't be said of everyone.

I believe more lives are spoiled by bitterness and a lack of forgiveness than anything else. And the longer we carry a grudge, the heavier it becomes. We cannot afford to harbor bitterness in our soul. The price we must pay is too great!

It isn't surprising that Christ warned His disciples on several occasions to forgive others. After teaching them how to pray, He declared: "'But if you do not forgive men their sins, your Father will not forgive your sins'" (Matthew 6:15, NIV). I don't pretend to know exactly what Christ meant by those words, but I do know that He commands us—for our own sake as well as for the sake of others—to forgive those who have offended and hurt us.

Paul reiterated this principle when he wrote: "Bear with each other and forgive whatever grievances you may have against one another. Forgive as the Lord forgave you" (Colossians 3:13, NIV).

LEARNING TO FORGET

After forgiving someone, forgetting is vital. Forgetting means making a commitment to that person that you will never hold that incident against him. In your mind, you view that person as if he had never offended you at all.

Joseph came to view his own brothers in that way. That's why he called his firstborn Manasseh, for "'God has made me forget all my trouble and all my father's household'" (Genesis 41:51, NIV). Joseph not only forgave his brothers, but he never held their wicked actions against them.

Clara Barton, the founder of the American Red Cross, was reminded one day of a vicious deed that someone had done to her years before. But she acted as if she had never even heard of the incident.

"Don't you remember it?" her friend asked.

"No," came Barton's reply, "I distinctly remember forgetting it."

We need to exhibit that same attitude toward the offenses which other people commit against us. But it isn't easy, as I learned while growing up. My father died when I was only ten years old. He left us quite a bit of property and some money, but his four brothers squandered everything we had. In three years my family was living in poverty and debt.

When I was older and really understood what they had done, I urged my mother to take revenge on them, to get a lawyer to take them to court and let them have it. The older I got, the more bitter I became.

But the Bible says, "Do not take revenge, my friends, but leave room for God's wrath, for it is written: 'It is mine to avenge; I will repay,' says the Lord" (Romans 12:19, NIV). He is the One who measures out justice. He wants to handle such judgment for us—perhaps now, certainly ultimately.

My mother always quoted verses such as Romans 12:19. She completely forgave my uncles for what they did. It took us twenty years to finish paying our debts, but she refused to become bitter. She forgot what they had done. Consequently, God gave her a freedom of spirit and opportunities to serve Him. God wants all of us to experience that same freedom and fruitfulness if we will only forgive others. The time came when I, too, forgave my uncles and determined not to hold their actions against them.

Is it time you buried someone else's past actions against you and forgot about the whole incident? Perhaps you feel bitter toward your father or mother. Maybe you're bitter toward a former professor or employer. You might even be bitter because someone broke his or her engagement to you. Whatever that person did, you feel you have reason enough to be bitter.

You may be thinking, "But why should I treat him decently after all he did to me? He has it coming." Look, if he has it coming, let the Lord lay it on. I tell you, there's no one like the Lord to let him have it if he needs it. Forgive and forget!

FORGIVING YOURSELF

As Christians we rejoice that our sins are forever washed away by Christ's blood. We marvel at God's infinite mercy to forgive us even though we don't deserve it. And by His grace we extend that forgiveness to others. But why is it that we won't forgive ourselves?

Oh, we know that "as far as the east is from the west, so far has he removed our transgressions from us" (Psalm 103:12, NIV). But from sunrise to sunset we needlessly carry a heavy burden of guilt.

For some reason we feel compelled to carry this burden, even though God never designed us that way. We need to learn to let go of our guilt.

Joseph's brothers had a hard time forgiving themselves. During the latter part of their lives—after their father, Jacob, had died—they feared for their lives. They couldn't believe that Joseph had really forgiven them. "Surely," they reasoned among themselves, "Joseph is waiting for Dad to die and then he's going to take revenge on us at last."

Joseph wept when he realized their concern and said, "'You intended to harm me, but God intended it for good...'" (Genesis 50:20, NIV).

Joseph could see the sovereign, merciful hand of God at work in his life. He had completely forgiven his brothers and forgotten their offense years before, and longed for them to experience that forgiveness themselves.

Have you learned to forgive yourself for your past failures? Have you purposefully tried to forget them after confession and restitution took place?

I don't know what you've done. I don't want to know. But I'm well aware that Satan has a thousand gimmicks to drag us into impurity. None of us has a clean track record.

Paul could tell a group of first century believers:

Neither the sexually immoral nor idolaters nor adulterers nor male prostitutes nor homosexual offenders nor thieves nor the greedy nor drunkards nor slanderers nor swindlers will inherit the kingdom of God. (1 Corinthians 6:9–10, NIV)

Then the apostle added:

And that is what some of you were. But you were washed, you were sanctified, you were justified in the name of the Lord Jesus Christ and by the Spirit of our God. (1 Corinthians 6:11, NIV)

Drink in those last phrases. Paul's point is that sinners, whatever their brand name, will not inherit the kingdom of God. But the Children of God will!

That's why the apostle John's words in 1 John 3:1 ring with excitement: "How great is the love the Father has lavished on us, that we should be called children of God! And that is what we are!" Are you a child of God? Will you inherit the kingdom of God? You can become a child of God by committing your life to Christ and believing that His death on the cross paid the penalty for all your sins—past, present, and future.

True, we don't fully know what it means to be children of God yet, but the day is coming when Christ will appear and we will at last be like Him.

Until we see the Savior face to face, our desire should be to keep ourselves pure, as He is pure. But we can't do that if we keep turning our head to look back at ugly attitudes or actions God has already forgiven and forgotten. For unless we learn to forget our sins, we will always live in that ugly past. Guilt will continue to eat away at us like a cancer.

Paul wasn't always an apostle. As Saul the zealous Pharisee he persecuted the church with a vengeance. He committed terrible sins. Yet afterward as a Christian he said, *"Forgetting what is behind and straining toward what is ahead, I press on toward the goal to win the prize for which God has called me heavenward in Christ Jesus"* (Philippians 3:13–14, NIV). He didn't dwell on his past failures. He buried them at the feet of Jesus and pressed onward.

We need to learn the same lesson today. If God has forgiven you, then certainly you can forgive yourself. If you have not yet confessed your sin to God and accepted His forgiveness, do it today. Commit your life to Christ. God *will* forgive your sins. And then forgive yourself. You must forgive yourself if you are to grow and experience the victorious Christian life to its fullest.

KEEPING SHORT ACCOUNTS

Forgive and be forgiven. And then forget it! This is the secret of spiritual health. Keep short accounts with God and men (Acts 24:16). Don't lock bitterness and guilt within some closet of your soul!

Allow the Holy Spirit to shine His divine spotlight in your heart. Let Him clean out every closet. Allow Him to free you from the bitterness you may feel toward someone else, or the guilt you may feel within yourself.

Then claim God's wonderful promise, "If we confess our sins, he is faithful and just and will forgive us our sins and purify us from all unrighteousness" (1 John 1:9).

May you experience His cleansing and healing today!

Struggling

with

Moral Purity

Charles R. Swindoll

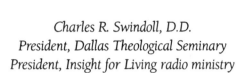

Charles R. Swindoll, D.D.
President, Dallas Theological Seminary
President, Insight for Living radio ministry
Author of nine Gold Medallion books

Holiness sounds scary. It need not be, but to the average American it is. Our tendency is to think that holiness would never find its way into the office of a salesperson; certainly not that of an aggressive and successful athletics coach. Nor would a mother of small children be that concerned about holiness, nor a teenager involved in a busy high school; to say nothing of some collegian pursuing a career with his or her eyes on great financial goals. Let's face it, holiness is something for the cloistered halls of a monastery. It needs organ music, long prayers, and religious-sounding chants. It hardly seems appropriate for those in the real world of the twentieth century. Author John White seems to agree with that.

> Have you ever gone fishing in a polluted river and hauled out an old shoe, a tea kettle or a rusty can? I get a similar sort of catch if I cast as a bait the word *holiness* into the murky depths of my mind. To my dismay I come up with such associations as:

thinness
hollow-eyed gauntness
beards
sandals
long robes
stone cells
no sex
no jokes
hair shirts
frequent cold baths
fasting
hours of prayer
wild rocky deserts
getting up at 4 A.M.
clean fingernails
stained glass
self-humiliation[1]

Is that the mental picture you have when you think of holiness? Most do. It's almost as though holiness is the private preserve of an austere group of monks, missionaries, mystics, and martyrs. But nothing could be further from the truth.

As a matter of fact, holiness *does* belong in the life of the teenager. Holiness *does* have a place in the office of the salesperson. It is, indeed, appropriate in the world of the up-to-date, aggressive, even successful individual.

I couldn't be in greater agreement with Chuck Colson's statement: "Holiness is the everyday business of every Christian. It evidences itself in the decisions we make and the things we do, hour by hour, day by day."[2]

The Fog: An Analysis of Today's Moral Scene

Before going any further, let's back off a few feet and get a little perspective on the moral scene today. To penetrate the fog will take some effort, I can assure you. Perhaps it will help to read the writings of a sixth-century B.C. prophet named Habakkuk. His name looks like a misprint, doesn't it? On the contrary, the man was a bold voice for holiness in a day of compromise. A misfit, perhaps, but no misprint. Had you lived in his day, you may have wondered about his sanity! He was the kind of man who just wouldn't "get in line." His world was corrupt, but he believed in personal purity, of all things! How strange…yet how significant! We may not be familiar with him, but we surely understand his times.

He's a man who was surrounded by a moral fog. His book is an ancient call for repentance. It is a holy cry to God for divine intervention. And it's not just a cry; it's more like a scream. He says:

> How long, O LORD, will I call for help,
> And Thou wilt not hear?
> I cry out to Thee, "Violence!"
> Yet Thou dost not save. (Habakkuk 1:2, NASB)

He saw immoral and brutal acts of violence. So, of course, he asked, "Why?" He also asked, "*How long?*" He struggled with God's lack of immediate action. Though the prophet prayed, God seemed unusually distant. "How long? Why?" The heavens were brass. "Why don't You act decisively? Why don't You unfold Your arms and get with it in this old, polluted world of ours? How long before you deliver Your people, Lord?" He continues:

> Why dost Thou make me see iniquity,
> And cause me to look on wickedness?
> Yes, destruction and violence are before me;
> Strife exists and contention arises.
> Therefore, the law is ignored
> And justice is never upheld.

For the wicked surround the righteous;
Therefore, justice comes out perverted. (Habakkuk
1:3–4, NASB)
Are thou not from everlasting,
O LORD, my God, my Holy One?
We will not die. (1:12a, NASB)

"I thought You were holy. Aren't You the Holy One? Then how
in the world can You sit back and do so little about my unholy
world?" "[Habakkuk] could not reconcile a bad world with a holy
God."3

How bad was his world? As we just observed, it was a world
of brutal violence (1:2) so severe that the prophet screamed out
his prayer. It was a world of personal iniquity and wickedness
(1:3). "Why dost Thou make me see *iniquity*?" The word includes
lying, vanity, and idolatry. "Why do You cause me to look on
wickedness?" That Hebrew term encompasses oppression, robbery,
and assault.

There were crimes of homicide going on in the streets. "Aren't
You Jehovah of Judah? Aren't You the God of this nation? Where
are You, God?"

There were strife and relational wrangling. There were arguments in homes, fights between parents and kids as well as
between marital partners—not to mention disputes between
bosses and employees. And did you notice another relevant issue?
The law was not being upheld. And when it was, it was being
compromised. What a scene! It's going to sound familiar: brutal
violence, personal iniquity, relational wrangling, legal compromise. You'd think Habakkuk lived in the inner city of some
American metropolis.

I smiled when I was listening to a rather well-known Bible
expositor several months ago. He said he'd just completed a serious study into the fourth, fifth, and sixth centuries B.C. and found
himself intrigued to discover what they wrestled with back then.

He mentioned five issues that concerned those ancient people: (1) the imminent outbreak of international hostility; (2) the breakup of homes—weakening marriages; (3) the rebellion of youth and their lack of respect for parents or for the elderly; (4) the corruption in politics—integrity was undermined; and (5) the chuckholes in the public roads!

Does that sound familiar? Does it sound like something you could identify with? History certainly has a way of repeating itself!

That's what makes Habakkuk's complaint so timely. "I thought you were holy, God! Where are You? How can You allow this to happen? I'm tired of breathing it in. I'm tired of its diseased impact on my life. I'm beginning to wonder about a holy God in a world of people *this* unholy." Maybe those are your sentiments too.

Habakkuk cried aloud. Another prophet named Jeremiah just quietly sobbed. I have in mind his words as recorded in Jeremiah 6. He lived a little later than Habakkuk, though not by much. Habakkuk feared the nation's demise, but Jeremiah lived to see the nation destroyed.

That's why he wrote Lamentations, which is another name for *weeping*. Appropriately, Jeremiah is called "the weeping prophet." He doesn't scream. He doesn't fight. He doesn't even argue. He just sobs. He writes his prophecy while wiping tears from his eyes.

> "Be warned, O Jerusalem,
> Lest I be alienated from you;
> Lest I make you a desolation,
> A land not inhabited." (Jeremiah 6:8, NASB)

Verse 10a:

> To whom shall I speak and give warning,
> That they may hear?
> Behold, their ears are closed....

Understand, that's the result of living in the fog. "The system" takes its toll. Your ears slowly become closed, so much so that you can't hear the spiritual message God is giving. *"They cannot listen."* Observe the way Jeremiah puts it:

> The word of the LORD has become a reproach to them;
> They have no delight in it. (6:10b, NASB)

Do you want to know how that sounds in today's terms? "Aw, c'mon...get off that stuff! Get up with the times, man! All that prophet-of-doom talk is old hat. This is where it's at!": In Jeremiah's words, *"They have no delight in it"*—that is, in hearing the truth about holiness.

> But I am full of the wrath of the LORD:
> I am weary with holding it in. (6:11a, NASB)

"I'm boiling. I'm churning...I'm so tired, Lord."

> "For from the least of them even to the greatest of them,
> Everyone is greedy for gain...." (6:13a, NASB)

Does that sound familiar?

Again, these verses describe life as it is lived in a moral fog. There is a constant fighting for gain. There's competition to get more and more. And to make matters worse:

> "From the prophet even to the priest
> Everyone deals falsely." (6:13b, NASB)

Jeremiah weeps, "It's bad enough that it's in the law courts, but it's now in the pulpits, my Lord. It's to the place where I can't trust the one who wears a collar, who says he speaks for You. I can't be sure that those who are robed with the mantle of God tell me the truth anymore. They deal falsely. They have healed the wound of Your people just slightly." Look at what he says! "They keep saying 'Shalom, shalom!' when there is no shalom! There isn't any peace. But they keep saying, 'Don't worry. Don't worry. It's gonna be OK,' when it's *not* going to be OK."

And if you don't think *that's* bad, look at verse 15.

> "Were they ashamed because of the abomination they have done?
> They were not even ashamed at all;
> They did not even know how to blush."

Honestly now, did you know the Bible spoke of a time in history when people were so caught up in an immoral lifestyle that they no longer blushed? Jeremiah sobs, "I notice, God, that there are no more red faces. No one seems shocked anymore."

Today I suppose we could call it compensating or maybe rationalizing. In order to handle the shock of our day, we compensate by remaining free of shock. I repeat, that's part of living in the fog.

Psychiatrist Karl Menninger took up the pen of a prophet when he wrote *Whatever Became of Sin?* In that searching book he admits, "In a discussion of the sin of *lust* we have to allow for a considerable shift in the social code during the past century. It has been called a revolution, and perhaps it is. Many forms of sexual activity which for centuries were considered reprehensible, immoral, and sinful *anywhere*, and their public exhibition simply *anathema*, are now talked and written about and exhibited on the stage and screen."[4]

From *Honesty, Morality, and Conscience* by Jerry White, I find a similar concern:

> We live in the age of freedom of expression and freedom of lifestyle. X-rated movies and magazines are available in

every city. Legislation to control pornography has failed in most places. The sexual fiction of yesterday is the reality of today. Magazines displayed in supermarkets present articles featuring unmarried couples living together. Sex manuals advocate extramarital affairs. Fewer and fewer teenagers leave high school as virgins. Prime-time television flaunts homosexuality and infidelity.[5]

Pitirim Sorokin, formerly professor of sociology at Harvard, laments:

There has been a growing preoccupation of our writers with the social sewers, the broken homes of disloyal parents and unloved children, the bedroom of the prostitute, a cannery row brothel, a den of criminals, a ward of the insane, a club of dishonest politicians, a street corner gang of teenage delinquents, a hate-laden prison, a crime-ridden waterfront, the courtroom of a dishonest judge, the sex adventures of urbanized cavemen and rapists, the loves of adulterers and fornicators, of masochists, sadists, prostitutes, mistresses, playboys. Juicy loves, ids, orgasms, and libidos are seductively prepared and served with all the trimmings.[6]

And to add Jeremiah's observation: Nobody blushes anymore. It's all part of the moral pollution…the fog. "The system" may be insidious, but it is effective.

In every major city today, with a turn of the television dial, you can bring explicit sex right into your home for anybody to watch. And nobody blushes.

You don't even have to go into an "adult" bookstore anymore to find pornography. You can find it in quick-stop grocery stores or in some large drugstores and supermarkets. You may have to look a little, but it's there. Again, I remind you, nobody blushes.

The ultimate, telltale sign of a low view of personal holiness is that we no longer blush when we find wrong. Instead, we make jokes about it. We re-dress immorality and make it appear funny. And if we don't laugh, we're considered prudes...we're kind of crotchety.

Maybe I don't like to laugh about that anymore because, as a minister, I am forced to deal with the consequences of it. And that's *never* funny. People in the backwash of a sensual lifestyle don't come to me and my staff to talk about the lasting joys of illicit sex. They wonder about their family; or what they should do about this disease; or now they can deal with this incestuous relationship that is tearing the home apart; or how they are going to tell their parents that she's pregnant out of wedlock, knowing it will break their parents' hearts.

It would be bad enough if it were limited to the world, but, as I mentioned in my introduction, it is now in the church—the place most people would consider to be the ultimate bastion of holiness.

The Truth: God's Timeless Counsel for Christians

I am grateful that God talks straight when it comes to moral purity. I'm grateful He doesn't stutter or shuffle or shift His position. I'm even more grateful that He doesn't laugh. It's as if He is looking His people directly in the eye and lovingly, yet firmly, saying, "I want you to hear this very clearly. I'll make it brief and simple." And He then leaves us with a decision regarding personal holiness. Only one decision pleases Him—*obedience.*

As John Brown, a nineteenth-century Scottish theologian, once stated: "*Holiness* does not consist in mystic speculations, enthusiastic fervors, or uncommanded austerities; *it consists in thinking as God thinks and willing as God wills.*"[7]

That's what the apostle Paul is asking of the reader in chapter 4 of 1 Thessalonians. He got his foot in the door in the last part of chapter 3 when he set forth a foundational guideline on how to *"really live"* as we *"stand firm in the Lord"* (3:8, NASB). And what does that include?

> And may the Lord cause you to increase and abound in love for one another, and for all men, just as we also do for you; so that He may establish your hearts unblamable in holiness. (3:12–13a, NASB)

What a great way to live—"unblamable in holiness"! Confident living is directly linked to being "unblamable." It's better than knowing the answers to all the questions on a test, or having plenty of money, or earning an advanced degree. There's no security like being free of blame. When we are established in holiness, living unblamable lives of moral purity, we can smile at life. We can take its pressures and enjoy its pleasures. And then when marriage comes along, we can enjoy the partnership of the opposite sex, including all the joys of sexual delights.

Make no mistake about it. God is pleased when married partners enjoy a healthy sex life in marriage. He applauds it. And why shouldn't He? He invented it. His Word clearly states that marriage is to be held in honor and that the marriage bed is to be undefiled—free of blame (Hebrews 13:4). But the implied warning is clear: If we remove sex from its original, God-given context, it becomes "sexual immorality," "lustful passion," and "impurity."

IN YOUR WALK, EXCEL!

1 Thessalonians 4:1–2

> Finally then, brethren, we request and exhort you in the Lord Jesus, that, as you received from us instruction as to how you ought to walk and please God (just as you actually do walk), that you may excel still more. (4:1, NASB)

We have other ways of saying "excel" today: "Go for it. Give it your best shot. Don't just drift; pursue!" Or, as many parents often say, "Get with it!" Paul says, in effect, "just as we have written you and have served as models before you, I encourage you to excel in your walk. *Get with it!* Make something happen in your life. Don't just drift along in a fog of mediocrity. Go the second mile. Excel!"

If you're a C student, try your best for a B. If you tend to be rather laid back in life, now is the time to go beyond your normal level. I exhort you to give yourself to diligence. Overcome that tendency toward laziness. All of that and more is involved in excelling.

While advocating an excelling lifestyle, Paul zooms in on one specific area that needs constant attention: moral purity.

IN YOUR MORALS, ABSTAIN!

1 Thessalonians 4:3–6

> For this is the will of God, your sanctification; that is, that you abstain from sexual immorality. (4:3, NASB)

Paul has written strong and emotional words regarding our spiritual walk. We are to excel in it. Now he specifies our moral life. Whoever wishes to excel in his or her spiritual walk must come to terms with an inner battle: sexual lust. Yes, it's a battle…a vicious, powerful, relentless fight that won't suddenly stop when we turn fifty. And it won't end just because we may lose our mate. Nor will it decrease because our geography changes, or because we are well educated, or because we may be isolated behind prison walls, or because we remain single, or even because we enter the ministry. The struggle to be morally pure is one of those issues from which no one is immune. That includes *you!* Now let's understand what God is saying here.

"This is the will of God." Very seldom will you find such

straight talk in Scripture. When it comes to remaining morally pure, you don't need to pray and ask whether it is God's will. "This is the will of God…abstain from sexual immorality." That last word is translated from the Greek word *porneia*. Obviously, we get our words *pornography* and *pornographic* from that original term. It refers to any kind of intimate, sexual encounter apart from one's marital partner. It would include, of course, intimate encounters with the opposite sex or with the same sex. Fornication, adultery, or homosexuality would be included in *porneia*. Clearly, the command is that we are to *abstain*. Abstain means exactly that—*abstain*. Outside marriage, have nothing to do with sexual involvements with others.

Now in the fog of horizontal standards, you will be left with any number of options. You will be told by some to be discreet, but certainly not to abstain. "I mean, let's not be fanatical about this." A few may even counsel you, "It would be dangerous for you to play around with somebody else's mate, so don't do that. And, for sure, you need to watch out for disease." But wait. Abstain, in Scripture, doesn't simply mean "watch out" or "be discreet." It means "have *nothing* to do" with something. Others' advice continues: "It's unwise for you to cohabit with a partner in your family. That's incest." (It is not only unhealthy, but it is illegal.) "If you're a teacher, you shouldn't be intimate with your students. That's not professionally wise, so don't do that," some would caution. But again I remind you: Scripture clearly states that it is God's will that we abstain. Moral purity is a matter of abstaining, not simply being careful.

How relieving it is to know exactly where we stand with our holy God! Now then, let's be very specific: If you are not married, there are no sexual exceptions provided for you. It is the will of God that you not be sexually intimate with any other person until marriage. That's what Scripture teaches both here and elsewhere. That is how to walk in obedience. It is God's best. Furthermore, it is for our good and it enhances God's glory.

I am pleased to add that we are not left with simply a stark command. Amplifying counsel follows in verses 4 and 5:

That each of you know how to possess his own vessel in sanctification and honor, not in lustful passion, like the Gentiles who do not know God.

It is God's will that we abstain from moral impurity. It is *also* His will that we know how to do that. I suggest that you must become a student of *yourself* in order to know how to handle your battle with sexual lust. Those who fail to know themselves will lose the battle and ultimately become enslaved to lust. In order for one to "possess his own vessel," there must be a practical, working knowledge of one's own tendencies.

You know what kind of student you are, academically, in order to pass the course. You have to apply what you know will work in order to pass the test, and accomplish the course, and get the degree or the diploma, correct? In the realm of your intimate life, there must be another equally diligent application of knowledge. Each of us is to know how to "possess his own vessel"—meaning, maintain purity in one's own body.

The point? In order to abstain from *porneia,* we must become alert and disciplined students of our bodies; how they function, what appeals to them, and what weakens as well as strengthens them. We are to know how to control our inner drive, how to gain mastery over it, and how to sustain ourselves in a life of purity rather than yielding to lustful passions.

Let me amplify that by putting it in practical words no one can possibly misunderstand. Within the media there are certain things that you and I cannot handle. We are to know ourselves well enough to admit that and to face the fact that certain sensual stimuli weaken us. We simply cannot tolerate those things and stay pure. The obvious conclusion is this: We are wrong to traffic in them. There are certain magazines you and I should not read.

There are certain films, television programs, and late-night channels we have no business watching. There are certain people who, by their suggestive conversations, weaken us. There are settings too tempting, touches too personal, and liberties that are too much for us to handle. We are fools to play around with them. They create appealing temptations we simply cannot control. So, if we are committed to abstain, we stay clear of them.

Such decisions are difficult to make and even more difficult to implement, but it is all part of our knowing how to "possess [our vessels] in sanctification and honor." Remember this: No one automatically remains morally pure. Abstention from sexual immorality is never an easy-come, easy-go issue. As I said earlier, it's a battle. We're talking *warfare!*

The battle rages in the realm of sexually stimulating activities. Even some parties, places, kinds of music, and pastimes can weaken us. Again, we are fools to tolerate those things. A person who is trying to recover from alcoholism realizes he is fighting a losing battle if he chooses to live on the second floor above a bar. No question about it, it will lead to failure. There is more:

> And that no man transgress and defraud his brother in the matter because the Lord is the avenger in all these things, just as we also told you before and solemnly warned you. (4:6, NASB)

Some would get around total sexual abstention by saying, "Well, what we could do is just keep this within the family. It's OK if it's between two family members or among Christians." But He corners us here as well. He adds that "no [one] transgress and defraud his brother in the matter because the Lord is the avenger in all these things."

This verse refers not only to members in the family of God but to individual family members—the indecent practices of relating intimately to one's daughter or daughter-in-law, son or son-in-law, mother, stepmother, father, stepfather, and on and on, covering the whole realm of incest. Such indecent, unlawful acts defraud our family members!

Now to state it painfully straight: God clearly and unequivocally stands against extramarital sex, homosexual sex, and sexual encounters with individuals outside of marriage under ANY situation. I repeat the command is direct and dogmatic: "Abstain from sexual immorality."

As I write this, I realize I am not the only one saying these things. But, I confess, sometimes I feel like a lonely voice in our day. And because some illustrations could appear as gossip, I choose not to use anyone else but myself as an example. Allow me to tell you *my* story.

My wife and I were married in June of 1955. We both were quite young. I finished my schooling and then faced the need to fulfill my military obligation. Back in the 1950s the military was not an option to choose but a requirement to be fulfilled. Because their time requirement best suited my particular situation, I chose the Marine Corps...an outfit not known for its moral purity.

I received the promise from my recruiting officer that if I joined, I would not have to serve my military duty overseas. And since I was married, that certainly was appealing to me because I was enjoying life with my bride, and the last thing we wanted was a forced separation from each other. I really wanted to be with her. But, through a chain of events too lengthy to explain, I wound up eight thousand miles from home. Stationed in the Orient for over a year, I was suddenly faced with sexual temptation as I had never known it.

Before I ever dropped the seabag off my shoulder on the island of Okinawa, I was faced with a tough decision. I was going to make my home in a barrack that was characterized by a godless lifestyle. Venereal disease was not uncommon among those on the island. Living with a woman in the village was as common as breathing smog in Southern California. If you lived in Okinawa, you slept around. And it wasn't uncommon for the chaplain, who was supposed to lecture incoming marines about purity, to ultimately joke his way through and tell you where to go to get penicillin shots. Welcome to the real world, Swindoll.

I realized, especially since I had known the joys of intimacy in marriage, that temptation would be incredibly strong. Surrounded by men who couldn't have cared less about the things of God, away from my home and free from physical accountability to my wife and my family, I would soon become another nameless marine on the back streets of Okinawan villages. But I was a Christian. I determined then and there to "abstain from sexual immorality." How I praise my Lord for His sustaining strength!

By the grace of God, the decision that I made back in the late 1950s allows me to speak and write today with confidence. Had I not been preserved from unfaithfulness, I would have to pass rather hurriedly and embarrassingly over this passage and similar sections of Scripture. I sincerely doubt that I would have pursued the ministry had I fallen into sexual lust.

Candidly, I had to be tough on myself. There were times when I had to be downright *brutal* with my emotions. I had to make some tough, Spartan decisions...unpopular decisions among a bunch of guys who tried everything in the book to tempt me. I was determined to be different so that I could reach those fellow marines with a message that had integrity. Let me clarify something, lest you misunderstand. God showed me it wasn't my job to clean up the goldfish bowl; it was my job to fish. I wasn't called to lead a flag-waving crusade for moral purity across the Orient. It was my job to live clean whether anybody else did or not. To put it bluntly, I was not to put my hands on someone who wasn't my wife. I wasn't even to *talk* about such things. Today I can speak from experience when I write these words: Sexual abstention works. It pays rich and rewarding dividends. It works...even in the life of a young, red-blooded marine surrounded by endless opportunities to yield.

And God made it clear to me that if I would abstain from sexual immorality, He would honor that. And His Spirit came to my rescue time and again. I had no corner on strength. I was often in the path of temptation, as anyone reading these words right now would understand, but I refused to surrender. Those were lonely days away from home for almost eighteen months. I was often burning with desire for my wife. But, thank God, I was committed to abstaining from immorality.

How did I make it? I involved myself in things that were wholesome, things that paid off, things that kept me busy, active, and fulfilled. I cultivated my musical abilities by becoming much more proficient in several instruments. I also was involved in an aggressive athletic program, spending most of my spare time with men who were committed to the same wholesome objectives. In my mind, the village was "off limits." I didn't even drop in and get a soft drink in the village bars. I couldn't handle it. When I got off the bus that took me to my destination, I looked straight ahead and walked fast. That little island had physically attractive women and over five thousand places of prostitution. I never touched one of them. Obviously, I saw them...but I refused to yield.

In my heart I knew that once I broke, once I stepped into that sensual world, I would not stop. I knew the drive that was inside me couldn't be stopped once I yielded. And I probably would not even have wanted to stop it. It's like breaking with a diet. Once you take off the restraint, it's much easier to say, "Who cares?" Once you've eaten a little chocolate cake following lunch, that night it's *half a pie!*

Perhaps you are thinking, "That just mocks me, because my lifestyle isn't there. I've compromised sexually...I'm not walking in purity." Wait! My message to you isn't complicated—*start today!* It's time to take charge, my Christian friend. Telling yourself it won't work is the very thing that keeps you from a life of moral purity and its rewards. Stop lying to yourself! If you are born from above, if you are a child of God, then this passage is addressed to *you*. Your name belongs at the beginning of these verses.

See verse 1 of 1 Thessalonians 4? "Finally then, *brethren*..." Put your name there. This is specific instruction for you, child of God. No one else has the power. To be very frank with you, it's beyond me how an unsaved person can stay morally pure. Only by the power of the living Christ and His Spirit can this kind of life be carried out. If you really want to live in moral purity, yet you are not a Christian, then put first things first. You need to come to Christ. Becoming a Christian precedes cleaning up your moral act. Trusting in the Lord Jesus Christ is primary. Only then can you call upon the power you will need to walk in personal holiness.

Even then, I remind you, it won't be easy or automatic. You'll still need to apply the techniques I've mentioned to sustain your commitment to purity. I have found there are times when temptation is so fierce I have to be almost rude to the opposite sex. That may not sound very nice, but that's the price I'm willing to pay. It's worth it, believe me.

Some of you are husbands and fathers. The habits of fidelity you are forming directly affect your wife and children at home. How careful are you with personal holiness? How consistent? How tough are you on yourself? You cannot depend on anyone else to provide you with a moral standard. YOUR moral standard is the one that's going to keep you pure...or lead you astray. Isn't it time you became serious about moral purity?

You may be single, attractive, and capable. You may have entered a fine career. That's great...but it is also possible that you have begun to compromise your morals. You may find yourself saying, "It feels so good, and I am so lonely, and it is so accessible, so secret." Wait...it *isn't* secret! There is no "secret sin" before God. Furthermore, it won't remain a secret on earth forever.

See what it says in verse 6? It's not often that the Lord calls Himself the *Avenger*, but He does in this case. The meaning? "One who satisfies justice by punishing or disciplining the wrongdoer."

Not all of that avenging will wait until the judgment day. Some of it happens now in the form of anxiety, conflict, guilt, disease, insanity...even death.

By the way, 1 Corinthians 6:18 is a pretty significant verse. In a context much like the one we've been considering, the writer exhorts the reader not to compromise morally. The verse says:

> Flee immorality. Every other sin that a man commits is outside the body, but the immoral man sins against his own body.

Practically speaking, all other sins can be fairly well managed in an objective manner. But this one comes in on you. In today's terms, it's an "inside job." In many ways, sexual sins take a personal toll on the victim, leaving the person in bondage, increasingly less satisfied, and on a downward spiral which only results in greater tragedy.

Few have ever said it better than Evangelist Billy Graham:

> In every area of our social life we see operating the inevitable law of diminishing returns in our obsession with sex. Many do something for a thrill only to find the next time that they must increase the dose to produce the same thrill only to find the next time that they must increase the dose to produce the same thrill. As the kick wears off, they are driven to look for new means, for different experiences to produce a comparable kick. The sex glutton is tormented by feelings of guilt and remorse. His mode of living is saturated with intense strain, unnatural emotions, and inner conflicts. His personality is thwarted in its search for development. His passions are out of control, and the end result is frustration. In his defiance of God's law and society's norm, he puts a death-dealing tension on his soul. His search for new thrills, for new

kicks, for exciting experiences keeps him in the grip of fear, insecurity, doubt, and futility. Dr. Sorokin says: "The weakened physical, emotional, and spiritual condition of the sex glutton usually makes him incapable of resisting the accompanying pressures, and he eventually cracks under their weight. He often ends by becoming a psychoneurotic or a suicide."[8]

When just a small boy, I remember memorizing the following:

Sow a thought, and you reap an act;
Sow an act, and you reap a habit;
Sow a habit, and you reap a character;
Sow a character, and you reap a destiny.

How true! And we never come to the place where we can call a halt to the sowing-reaping process.

I heard of a Christian leader who interviewed a veteran missionary who was then in his eighties. The interviewer asked, "Tell me, when did you get beyond the problem with lust?" In candor the godly gentleman answered, "It hasn't happened yet. The battle still goes on!" If you're waiting to outgrow the battle, don't hold your breath.

IN YOUR REASONING, REMEMBER!

1 Thessalonians 4:7–8

For God has not called us for the purpose of impurity, but in sanctification. (4:7, NASB)

Paul uses "sanctification" for the third time in this passage. It's a theological term referring to our pilgrimage, our progress from earth to heaven. Perhaps we could call it our growth pattern.

Remember this: You and I have been called to operate in the sphere of spiritual progress. God has called us to be in a spiritual growth pattern. Sometimes we're up...sometimes down. Sometimes we're more victorious than other times. But the progress is a movement forward and higher. God certainly has *not* called us for the purpose of impurity, even though we continue to live in a world socked in by a moral fog.

> Consequently, he who rejects this is not rejecting man but the God who gives His Holy Spirit to you. (4:8, NASB)

The second thing to remember is: To reject a lifestyle of holiness is to reject the God who empowers you to live it. Holy living is inseparably linked to believing in a holy God.

The Choice: A Decision Only You Can Make

Let me conclude my thoughts by simplifying your options. Actually, you have two. First, you can choose to live your life in a horizontal fog. If that is your choice, the results are predictable. You will continue to drift in a fog of moral uncertainties. Your disobedience will result in a series of rationalizations that will leave you empty. Guilt and grief will be your companions. You can choose to live like that. If you do, you open up a door of misery for yourself. You'll play at church. You'll toss around a few religious words. But before very long, your lifestyle will match the atmosphere around you. Your eyes will no longer tear up. Your conscience will no longer sting. Your heart won't beat faster. You may even stop blushing. A jaded, horizontal lifestyle is an option. But it has those consequences...those terrible consequences.

Why? The Avenger. God doesn't let His children play in the traffic without getting hurt. Your disobedience will result in increasing personal misery.

Second, you can choose to live your life vertically on target. The benefits? You will honor the God of moral absolutes. And your obedience will result in greater personal confidence and habits of holiness. It will begin to come supernaturally. You'll find yourself stronger, more secure, possessing a healthy self-image.

Internally, we're a little like an automobile. The God who made us built us with all the right lights on our internal dashboard. I don't know of anybody who after purchasing a new car also buys a little hammer for the glove compartment. Let's imagine a weird scene. Let's say that as two men are driving along, one of the lights on the dashboard starts flashing red. The driver says to his friend, "Hand me that hammer in the glove compartment. OK? Thanks." Tap...Tap...Bamm...Bamm...Pow! "There! Now we've gotten right of *that* light." Smoke is coming out of the hood, yet the guy keeps driving along.

How foolish! And yet, it isn't difficult to find people who will hand out hammers. As they do, they say, "Aw, that's needless guilt. We're in an age where guilt is no longer considered important. You need to get rid of all that stuff." But wait...that's NECESSARY guilt! God help us when we don't have it! It's the conscience that bites into us deep within and stings us when we compromise our moral purity. When we sin, it's *supposed* to hurt. We are *supposed* to be miserable when we compromise morality. That's the red light flashing down inside. It's God's way of saying, "Pull over...stop. Lift the hood. Deal with the real problem."

Jonathan Edwards, one of the great preachers of early American history, once made this resolution: *"Resolved,* Never to do any thing, which I should be afraid to do if it were the last hour of my life."[9]

You have available to you the power that's necessary to solve the real problems of your life. He is Jesus Christ. And once you have the Savior, you also have the Holy Spirit. He will come inside not to mock you but to help you; not simply to cry with you over how strong the temptation is but to empower you to overcome it. You can do all things through Him who keeps on pouring His power into you. Even if you have never done it in your life, you can begin a life of power today. There's no checklist. There's no probation period. There's no long list of responsibilities that you must fulfill before God will give you the power. If you've never met the Savior, holiness begins at the cross, where Christ paid the penalty for sin. Take Him now.

1. John White, *The Fight* (Downers Grove, Ill.: InterVarsity Press, 1976), 179.

2. Charles W. Colson, *Loving God* (Grand Rapids, Mich.: Zondervan Publishing House, 1983), 131.

3. Kyle Yates, *Preaching from the Prophets* (North Nashville, Tenn.: Broadman Press, 1953), 152.

4. Karl Menninger, *Whatever Became of Sin?* (New York: Bantam Books, Inc., 1978), 138.

5. Jerry White, *Honesty, Morality, and Conscience* (Colorado Springs, Colo.: NavPress, 1979), 184.

6. Billy Graham, *World Aflame* (New York: Doubleday & Co., Inc., 1965), 21–22.

7. John Brown, *Expository Discourses on 1 Peter* (Edinburgh: Banner of Truth, reprint edition, 1848), 1:106. Italics in original.

8. Billy Graham, *World Aflame,* 23.

9. *The Works of Jonathan Edwards,* 2 vols., revised and corrected by Edward Hickman (Carlisle, Pa.: The Banner of Truth Trust, reprint edition, 1976), 1:XX. Italics in original.

STRUGGLING
WITH MARRIAGE

STEVE STEPHENS

Steve Stephens
Psychologist, author

It began with a little itch on his right leg. No big deal. A little scratch and the itch went away.

Several days later the itch returned and scratching only made it worse. He visited the doctor and the itch vanished after applying the prescribed medication. Before long, Mun Ki developed strange sensations in both legs. He cooked up an old home remedy and his legs felt much better.

A week later a sore irritated the big toe on his right foot. It grew and spread to the toes on both feet. He became pale and shivered in the warm weather. By now he knew the cause of his misery. He tried all sorts of treatment and medicines, but nothing slowed down the disease. Finally, Mun Ki was forced to admit there was no cure for leprosy.

Three months after the first symptoms appeared, Mun Ki sat with his wife and four children eating the evening meal. When the family finished eating, Nyuk Tsin, his wife, sent the children away. She knelt before her husband and said, "I shall be your *kokua*."[1]

This scene happens almost halfway through James Michener's epic novel *Hawaii*. In 1870 people diagnosed with leprosy were immediately banished to a leper colony on the island of Molokai.

The government's strategy was: out of sight, out of mind. The officials did allow one provision for comfort—a healthy individual, fully aware of their actions, could volunteer to accompany a victim to the leper colony. These people were called *kokuas,* the "helpers." The *kokuas* lived with and nursed the leper until one of them died. Then if the *kokua* had not contracted the disease, they were free to return to civilization.

To be a *kokua* took more than love and courage, it took true commitment. As each *kokua* boarded the ship that would take them to a voluntary exile, the police marshal asked carefully, "Are you sure you know what you are doing?"

Engaged couples need to consider that same question. Passion and excitement capture couples and they rarely slow down long enough to think about the ramifications of a genuine commitment. They stand before friends and relatives promising to be faithful through better or worse, richer or poorer, sickness or health, for the rest of their lives. The promise is solemn and those giving it are sincere. Commitments are easily given but it is difficult to live up to them,

When most of us were first married, we were grossly unprepared. There was so much we didn't know, and what is frightening is that we never realized how unprepared we actually were. Few of us even realized what those sacred words entailed. A wedding vow is no small thing. It is the initiation of a new relationship—husband and wife. It is a commitment that is both total and timeless. Yet at the heart of that commitment there is also an assumption of trustworthiness; for if a commitment is not trustworthy, then by definition it is neither total nor timeless. Without trust the vow is false and ultimately meaningless. So it is here that we must begin.

WHAT IS A TRUSTWORTHY COMMITMENT?

Trust is the bedrock on which to build the foundation of a marriage. A foundation must rest on something solid. A builder who does not dig deep and plant firm footings risks disaster. I once heard of a contractor who built a complex of expensive condominiums in an exclusive river-front development. The view was breathtaking, the architectural design received applause, and the choice of materials was top of the line. There was only one small problem. They built on unstable ground. Each year the complex slips an inch toward the river. That is not a fast rate, but in time these beautiful condominiums will collapse. Apparently the footing had been deep, but not deep enough to touch bedrock.

Eric Ericson, a well-known psychologist, writes that the first developmental task of children is "trust versus mistrust." Children learn early whether or not they can trust those around them. If they can, this sense of trust goes with them the rest of their lives. Yet if they can't, mistrust becomes their lifestyle.

All children yearn to trust. It's the basis of all future growth. Trusting is the ability to feel safe and secure. Without trust a person is unable to relax and reach beyond themselves. Life becomes a risk.

Here are a few of the situations that can steal away trust in childhood:

- Death of a parent
- Divorce of parents
- Physical or sexual abuse
- Neglect by parents
- Intense long-term conflict of parents
- Inconsistent discipline
- Lack of expressed love and warmth by parents
- Major trauma (e.g. death of a sibling, natural disasters, severe accidents, fire, hospitalizations)

These items block the development of security and can impact a person for the rest of his or her life. A damaged childhood trust makes it more difficult to trust as an adult. However, this trait can be reestablished if both partners are patient and trustworthy. In courtship the establishment of trust is critical and in marriage the continuation of that trust is equally critical. We build trustworthy commitments with honesty, dependability, and faithfulness. Let's look at each.

Honesty

Integrity is the core of any intimate relationship. To either state or imply that something is true, when in reality it is not, destroys trust. If we discover our spouse lies in one area, we tend to question them in all areas. We no longer believe what they tell us. Our trust is gone. We can't trust one who is dishonest.

Dependability

When someone is dependable we can relax. We don't need to worry or be afraid. In a dependable marriage, we can count on our spouse—we know they will be there when we need them. We base this dependability on a number of assumptions:

- Our spouse cares about us.
- Our spouse is concerned with our best interests.
- Our spouse won't maliciously hurt us.
- Our spouse is responsible.

If we question any of these four assumptions, we tend to pull back and be cautious. When a partner is undependable, we quickly learn that trust leads to disappointment.

Faithfulness

In marriage, faithfulness is a symbol of commitment. It is a statement that our heart belongs to our spouse. This loyalty takes precedence over all other allegiances—parents, relatives, co-workers, and friends of each gender. Faithfulness insists that we allow no one to compete with this special place of affection. Our partner is truly our one and only. Emotional or physical affairs are unthinkable when we have a faithful heart.

Marital trust is built over time. As our honesty, dependability, and faithfulness remain strong, our spouse sees us as trustworthy. However, there are four trust breakers that are so severe they destroy trust. These are not mere setbacks; they take one back to the beginning. Trust is more than damaged, it is annihilated. It no longer exists. They shatter either honesty, dependability, or faithfulness, and sometimes all three.

The following four trust breakers are critically important. To minimize them is to minimize a faulty foundation.

1. Abandonment
   (Emotional/Physical)
2. Abuse
   (Emotional/Physical/Sexual/Verbal)
3. Addictions
   (Alcohol/Drugs/Sexual)
4. Adultery
   (Emotional/Physical)

However, trust can be rebuilt if both partners are willing. It is not easy and it takes time. Wounds can heal, but trust breakers leave deep scars and threaten the future of a relationship. Anyone in a relationship where the above is currently happening should seek professional help immediately. Don't say, "It's no big deal," or "If I can hold on, it will get better." These four trust breakers are big deals and without help, situations tend to get worse.

When a couple comes to my office with a specific problem I often ask, "How long have you been aware of this difficulty?" It is not unusual for people to say, "Ten or twenty years."

"Why did it take you so long to seek help?"

"We just thought it would go away."

Problems don't just go away, they tend to get worse. They might start as a little seed, but given time they grow and grow and grow. Yet if we confront the problem early, there is hope.

Cindy was tired of Scott's late nights. She knew he had trouble with alcohol and that most of the nights he was at the local bar. When he stumbled in at 3:00 A.M., he apologized and promised he would never do it again. Cindy finally had enough of his empty promises. She confronted him with two choices: either he go into a month-long alcohol rehabilitation program or she was leaving.

"Do you really mean it?"

"Absolutely!"

"Okay, where do you want me to go?"

"St. Vincent's drug and alcohol unit has a bed waiting for you. I arranged it this morning."

"Let's go. If I'm going to do it I might as well get it over with."

Two years later, Scott is still sober with no relapse. Cindy says he is a new man and the marriage is better than ever. She has even learned to trust him all over again. With trust re-established, there can be a sincere commitment.

If there is no trust in the beginning, the original commitment is on a false foundation. If the trust is present at the beginning but broken later, the initial commitment is drained of meaning. The marriage may have the appearance of commitment but its spirit is severely wounded. Unless the trust is recaptured, the commitment is merely a social and financial illusion.

WHAT IS A TOTAL COMMITMENT?

Tonya and Sid were the perfect couple—young, attractive, intelligent, and deeply committed to God. They had been married less than two years when a drunk driver hit their car broadside. Sid walked away without a scratch. Tonya was unconscious with severe head injuries. She was rushed to the hospital and was in surgery for six hours. When she came to, the right side of her body was paralyzed and she could hardly speak. Sid propped pillows behind her head and placed a straw between her cracked lips so she could drink.

Three weeks later Tonya was released from the hospital. The doctors said the paralysis was permanent and she would be confined to a wheelchair. She couldn't walk or feed herself; her speech was slow and slurred; she couldn't even go to the bathroom without assistance.

As Sid sat in my office he looked exhausted and my heart went out to him.

"I love Tonya," he said, "but this isn't what I expected out of marriage. One minute we were happy and carefree, the next she's an invalid. This isn't fair! She's not the same person I married."

During the next few weeks Tonya's situation worsened. Terrible headaches kept her bedridden. Her right arm and leg atrophied into awkward and unusable positions. Discouragement and pain pulled Tonya deeper into herself as friends and relatives stopped visiting. It was just too hard to see Tonya in this state.

When I saw her, her face twitched as she slowly tried to articulate her thoughts. She told me she couldn't read anymore and it was hard to concentrate on what she heard.

"The only way I make it through my day is to repeat to myself different Bible verses I memorized as a child. Over and over I repeat them and pray that God will take me home." Then she gave me a strange look and her voice softened. "I told Sid to leave me, but he won't. Do you know what he said?"

I shook my head.

"He said he loved me and he'd never leave."

Her eyes filled with tears as she looked beyond me to something only she could see. "Isn't he crazy?" A tear fell down her cheek.

I grabbed a tissue and gently wiped the tear away. "No, he's not crazy. He's committed—totally committed."

Most of us aren't called to give as much as Sid.

Total commitment is the willingness to share everything—especially ourselves. Each of us is to give all of ourself to all of our spouse. Life is no longer a solo journey, but a joint endeavor. Two people giving themselves freely and equally of everything they can, fulfills the spirit of total commitment.

In this type of commitment we share our time, our possessions, and most significantly, our personhood. We give all we can—with no holding back. We reach deep into our soul to share emotions, beliefs, needs, traits, history, and dreams.

Total commitment is so broad that it is hard to focus in on the specifics, but our strengths and our sexuality are two specific areas we need to share with our spouse. Though these are just two of many critical areas to commit to each other, they do provide a place to begin.

Strengths

We are hesitant to discuss our strengths because we think it is arrogant or presumptive. However, since they are God given and we have nothing to do with it, we should not engage in such thinking. Rather, we need to acknowledge and understand our strengths so we can use them to enhance life with our spouse.

Usually, each of us excels in one or two of these areas and we are slightly retarded in one or two. In other words, we all have both strengths and weaknesses and both are part of the marital commitment. We need to know each other's strengths in order to encourage and build one another up in those areas. We also need to know each other's weaknesses so we can be understanding and compensate for them.

To be committed means to give who we are and part of who we are involves the following ten areas of intellectual strength:[2]

Verbal Intelligence. This is the ability to put one's thoughts into words. Writers, poets, and public speakers can express themselves in language, finding the right word for the right situation. My six-year-old daughter has good verbal intelligence. One evening I came home from work and said, "Brittany, you sure look beautiful."

"Daddy, I do not."

Taken back by her response, I asked, "What do you mean?"

"Look at my nose. It's runny and runny noses are not beautiful." There wasn't anything else I could think to say.

Mathematical Intelligence. People with this ability love numbers. They do not need calculators to add, subtract, multiply, or even divide. Calculations come naturally to them. They snicker at those of us who have math phobias or who struggle in this area.

People laugh when they hear how I deal with my checkbook. I have two strategies that simplify my accounting. First, I round everything up to the next dollar. Second, I have a special line item every month. It's called *Bank Adjustment*. When I get my statement from the bank, I compare what they say I have with what my ledger says and adjust it to what the bank says. I figure they must know what they are doing. One month the bank said I had four hundred dollars more than I had calculated, so I added it to my total. Tami and I celebrated. Then the next month the bank indicated they had made an error and took back the four hundred. We ate macaroni and cheese for the next thirty days.

Visual Intelligence. This ability involves seeing size, shapes, angles, distance, and perspective. It also involves seeing the interaction between objects. Some with good visual intelligence can even discern subtle hues of color and shadow. Artists, architects, and carpenters have visual intelligence.

My father has visual intelligence. He can look at a wall and say, "That's about seventeen-and-a-half feet long." I pull out my tape measure and he is right; seventeen-and-a-half feet.

This ability makes me very nervous when he parallel parks. We drive along and he says, "There's a spot!" I insist that we will never fit. He laughs and says, "There's at least a foot." I hold my breath as the car squeezes into the space, almost scratching the cars in front and back. Most people would never attempt this feat, but my father not only tries it, he does it without even slowing down. "Don't worry," he says, "there's plenty of room."

When the car finally stops and I can breathe again, I check the front and back bumper. Dad was right. There was a foot to spare—six inches in the front and six in the back.

Musical Intelligence. I envy those with the ability to sing and play instruments. Some read music and others can play by ear. My parents insisted that I take four years of piano lessons in hopes that I might develop some musical ability, but it didn't work. Meanwhile, my brother Dale, who never had any piano lessons, can sit at the piano and reproduce almost anything he has ever heard. He has musical intelligence.

Music is a wonderful ability which God did not grant me. Now I love to sing—in the shower, driving in the car, or playing with my children. I'm always singing. I don't always remember the words or have the tune correct so I make up something.

Our children quickly picked up my love for music. Unfortunately, they rarely have the words or tunes correct either. We sing our own versions of popular songs. My wife just sits and shakes her head when Brittany sings, "Row, row, row the car," or "Mary had a little dog."

Mechanical Intelligence. This is the ability to use one's hands to fix things. Mechanics, plumbers, electricians, and repairmen usually have this ability. Traditionally it's a man's field, but if something breaks down in our home, I rarely know what to do. My grandmother once told me you only need one tool to fix things—a hammer. If something doesn't work, you just start tapping it until it does.

My wife has better mechanical intelligence than I do. If the garbage disposal breaks, I will run to the garage for the hammer while she tears it apart, and before I know it, it's fixed.

Another part of mechanical intelligence is putting things

together. Tami and I will purchase a simple little toy for the children, and when we open the box there are hundreds of pieces and a fifty-step guide to assembly. I'm a fairly intelligent human being, but these instructions rarely make sense to me. Within fifteen minutes I'm so frustrated I have to take a short time-out. Then along comes Tami, she reads the instructions and quickly puts the whole thing together. I'm sure glad I have a wife with mechanical intelligence.

Logical Intelligence. Problem solving, troubleshooting, and thinking in a sequential manner is all a part of this ability.

Corporate executives, business administrators, and anybody involved with management have logical intelligence. These people think clearly from point A to point B to point C. All is in order and well structured. *Organization* is their middle name. They keep the world running smoothly, but they also drive those of us who are less logical a little crazy. Have you ever gotten into an argument with someone who is totally logical? It's just not fair. Anyway, who said arguments had anything to do with logic? Besides, being logical doesn't always make that person right.

Physical Intelligence. Dancers, athletes, and actors all have this ability. They are aware of their body. They can control and coordinate it with strength, grace, and expression.

My three children, at least at this point in their lives, do not have physical intelligence. They trip, run into walls, lose their balance, fall off chairs, bump their heads, and skin their knees.

My wife, on the other hand, was a gymnast and has great coordination. Several years ago our community had a strong wind storm and we lost some of the shingles on the roof. The next day I asked my wife to hold the ladder while I climbed up and replaced them. Once on top of the roof I had a hard time getting to the right spot. The shingles were slippery and the pitch was steep. I carefully crawled on my hands and knees up the roof—

two feet forward, then I would slip back two feet. After about fifteen minutes of absolutely no progress, Tami called up and suggested she give it a try. I gladly traded places thinking, *Does she really think she can do any better?* Well, she did. Tami stood up, got her balance, confidently walked up the steep pitch, and replaced the shingles.

Personal Intelligence. The person with this ability is in touch with their feelings, needs, and motives. In an attempt to better understand themselves they study psychology. Their world is inward and at times introspective as they ponder who they are and why they are that way. A psychotherapist once wrote about having a memory that "was accompanied by a good deal of emotion."[3] It involved building little houses and castles with stones. To fully understand why he had this strong feeling, he went to the beach every afternoon for a number of months and built little houses in the sand. In this way he hoped to recapture the events of his childhood that produced this emotion and, therefore, know himself a little better. This displayed personal intelligence.

My daughter, Brittany, may have it as well. When she had just turned two, my wife left her with me for the afternoon. We were playing and having a wonderful time when suddenly Brittany disappeared. I looked all over for her and finally found her in her closet, curled up with her blanket, her favorite doll, and a pacifier. In surprise I asked, "Brittany, what are you doing in your closet?" She pulled out her pacifier and said, "Daddy, I was getting a little stressed and I needed a break."

Social Intelligence. This is the ability to bring people together and help them feel relaxed. They can make a group laugh or organize them into action. People naturally gravitate to those blessed with social intelligence. This person might be an up-front type leader, but they might just as likely be a behind-the-scenes type person.

Everybody likes Sam. The party doesn't start until he arrives.

He is a natural mingler. If Sam is around, people have a good time. Sam is also the type of person you can call if there is a problem. He always seems to know the right thing to say. When you talk, Sam gives you all his attention and you sense he really cares. He even sends me a birthday card every year. Sam definitely knows how to deal with people.

Spiritual Intelligence. Some people have a special sense of good and evil. They have an awareness of God and the intangible forces of the universe. Those with spiritual intelligence have an extra measure of faith and can see beyond what is visible. This ability is possible for more than saints and mystics. It is also possible for everyday people such as you and me.

George was a successful physician working at a prestigious hospital who felt called by God to be a medical missionary. He knew God would take care of him and felt that if God said go, he should go.

Once in a while, when I meet a particular person or am in a certain situation, a shiver goes up my back and I get a definite sense of evil. I can't rationally explain this, but I believe it's a part of spiritual intelligence.

Sharing our strengths along with our weaknesses is an important part of marriage. It's the commitment of both our best and worst qualities that makes our vows so meaningful. It is easy to commit to the positive aspects of people—those admirable characteristics that everybody loves and respects. However, a commitment of the total person also involves those negative aspects we wish did not exist. Just ask Tonya and Sid.

Talk to each other about your strengths and weaknesses. Commit yourself to help build up your partner's strong areas by encouraging them to be everything God made them to be. Also, commit to protect and help compensate for your partner's weak areas—promising never to ridicule or use these areas against them.

Sexuality

Sexual intercourse is the consummation of the marriage commitment. It's the symbol of marital completeness. If there is no intercourse, a marriage may be annulled. The ceremony does not count if the commitment isn't total.

No marriage can exist totally isolated from the issue of human sexuality. Partners may be either embarrassed or obsessed by the subject, but it can't be ignored. To some it is a god and to others it is a demon. All of us are sexual beings; it is a part of who we are. Sex is neither sacred nor profane. It is simply a part of life.[4] Unfortunately, many couples see intercourse as merely a sexual act. They miss the power and significance of sexuality to a healthy marriage.

Sexual intercourse has four levels of meaning: reproduction, pleasure, communication, and unity.

Reproduction. Some couples see reproduction as an unwanted side-effect of sexual intercourse. People use pills, birth-control devices, wishful thinking, and abortions to avoid childbirth. Tami and I tried for over two years to have a child. Three emotional miscarriages left us both very aware of the miracle of birth. Reproduction is miraculous. That a male and female can come together sexually and produce a child is beyond words.

Tami's fourth pregnancy went full term. At 4:30 A.M. she woke me and said, "I think I'm ready." We jumped into the car and sped to the hospital. On the way, I turned to Tami and said, "Life will never be the same after today." I was right.

When Brittany's head crested I was curious and amazed. When she slid out and her pink chin quivered with her first cry, I was so ecstatic that tears streamed down my cheeks. There is nothing as awe-inspiring as watching the birth of a child.

Two years later, I was at the same hospital. Once more I was experiencing that wonderful ecstasy as I watched the delivery of our second child, Dylan. I had a son! My joy was suddenly clouded with alarm as I looked at a very blue baby. I looked at the physician and saw his troubled face. Then I realized Dylan had not cried. He was just lying there. Panic gripped me. My thoughts screamed, *What's wrong? Do something! Get him air!* The physician pushed on the baby's chest and Dylan let out a cry. The most wonderful cry I have ever heard.

Children are a blessing. Sexual intercourse is a joyous part of creating this blessing. It is a means of continuing the human race and guaranteeing that the stream of life will flow from generation to generation.

Saint Augustine, with many of the early church fathers, believed that reproduction was the only justification for sexual intercourse. However, a complete reading of the Holy Bible shows that God is interested in more than just the creation of babies. He is also concerned with the fulfillment of adults. Jesus said, "I am come that they might have life, and that they might have it more abundantly."[5]

Pleasure. Sexual intercourse is one of the most intense physical pleasures of life and it is important that its sheer delight be a part of marriage. When a husband and wife come together there is a celebration of human sexuality. However, this pleasure is not merely the biological release of energy and anxiety. It is also the result of two emotional factors:

1. **Giving.** This is where each partner seeks mutual pleasure, rather than just individual gratification. It is where the process of sharing satisfaction becomes as significant as the point of personal orgasm. The real fulfillment is wrapped up in the total joyous giving of one's self to another and the total joyous giving of another to oneself.

2. **Reaffirming.** Pleasure is gained from the reaffirmation of the original pledge of mutual love. Therefore the act of sexual intercourse takes on an element of psychological

satisfaction where our personhood is enhanced, romance is rekindled, and security is reinforced.

Every individual has desires and drives for sexual pleasure. The physical ecstasy, when truly shared, creates an emotional intimacy. The world outside the couple stops. Two individuals—body, soul, and spirit—are totally focused on each other. That is intense pleasure, plus a lot more that words can't even express.

Communication. The Hebrew word to describe intercourse is Yada meaning "to know" and it is a euphemism for the sex act.[6] This same word also describes intellectual and spiritual knowledge. In English, the word intercourse means "communication" and in a sense that is quite appropriate, for sexual intercourse is a special means of communication. Let's see how it provides a unique and intimate modality for mutual expression, exposure, and exploration.

> **1. Expression.** Someone once asked Mozart, "What are you trying to express by your music?" The famous artist replied, "If I could express it in words, I wouldn't need music."
>
> The marriage act is the means by which two people, committed to each other, can express the whole meaning and quality of their relationship. Sex extends the means through which a couple can communicate love and mutual concern. It enhances the meaning of marriage by becoming an expression of solidarity, intimacy, acceptance, affection, romance, and tenderness. It provides a language for the husband and wife not matched by words or any other act.
>
> **2. Exposure.** Sexual intercourse involves the opening up of ourselves to our partner. The nakedness alone is symbolic that nothing is hidden and that one is at a point of extreme personal vulnerability. For sexual intercourse to

be most meaningful, it requires the unhindered sharing of our innermost thoughts, feelings, and very being. This surrender of our private identity to another is both frightening and satisfying; for in the sexual relationship we willingly expose ourselves to the risk of rejection. To reveal oneself to another and to be trusted with that person's intimate self-revealing provides a new and deepened personal awareness that can both strengthen and complete one's identity. One's self-disclosure leads to the other's self-disclosure making this process truly reciprocal and, unless blocked, unending.

3. Exploration. Human sexuality provides knowledge of our mate. It is through the process of exploring the mystery of another person that we discover the mystery of ourselves. This desire for intimate involvement with another person inevitably leads to mutual growth. It draws a man and a woman toward each other in their search for understanding.

Communication is a necessity and communication through intercourse is one of the most meaningful experiences in marriage. The process of expression, exposure, and exploration within the context of sexuality allows and sustains a process of growth that should only get better as the anniversaries come and go.

Unity. Sexual intercourse brings together two total individuals and makes them one. The book of Genesis says, "Therefore shall a man leave his father and his mother, and shall cleave unto his wife; and they shall be one flesh."[7] To cleave to one's mate takes in every aspect of the relationship between husband and wife. It is through giving and receiving that two distinct personalities are considered one single unit. This solidarity involves the creation of a physical, social, mental, and spiritual unit.

1. Physical Unity. This is the most obvious manifestation of the one-flesh relationship. The intimate body contact, the tender sexual embrace, and the private meeting of male and female make the marriage act an intensely physical encounter. However, sexual intercourse is more than an encounter between two bodies. It is the reaching out of the spirit through the body, for nowhere do flesh and spirit touch so intimately. The body is essentially an epiphany of personhood and when it is given, so are all the secrets that it contains. Every instance of sexual intercourse is significant in itself; for the physical is inseparable from the totality of the oneness.

2. Social Unity. This is essential because it creates the promise of companionship. Loneliness is an awful thing. We all desire to share our hopes and fears, our joys and frustrations with one who understands. We want to belong and be taken from our isolation. Belonging has power and the one-flesh relationship is the most profound form of belonging. It is a companionship that requires and provides radical self-giving, unique self-exposure, and unrestrained self-commitment.

3. Mental Unity. It is impossible to consider the act of sexual intercourse apart from the mind, for the primary sex organ is the brain. The one-flesh relationship is an intimate blending that involves a unity of personality. Sexual intercourse is an expression of the individual. It is more than the meeting of two bodies, it is the meeting of two persons. Physical sexuality is the vehicle for the expression of psychological sexuality, yet the vehicle and the expression are so intertwined in the marriage act as to be virtually inseparable.

In sexual intercourse the most intimate aspects of two personalities touch and in this is created a union of two intellects, two emotions, and two wills. Isolate or exclude any one of these three from the physical union and the act runs the risk of being incomplete, meaningless, self-centered, or exploitive.

The intellect is needed to establish the proper attitude, the emotions to create the proper atmosphere, and the will to initiate the proper action. When an integration of this type takes place, a trust and surrender develop which cannot otherwise occur.

4. Spiritual Unity. We are all spiritual and sexual individuals. These two important aspects of our existence are closely related; both are private, unavoidable, and easily distorted. Sexual intercourse is symbolic of a commitment that has a specific spiritual dimension.

The marriage act is the sealing of a spiritual covenant with God and with our partner. It is an oath to God concerning our relationship to another. Therefore, the marriage covenant is a promise that only death can break. Sexual intercourse is a reaffirmation of the sincerity of that promise, but even more, for it is a statement about the couple. It states the existence of a permanent and exclusive commitment between two people. The faithfulness to this covenant involves the decision to stand together through and in spite of periods of conflict, struggle, boredom, and monotony. However, a total life commitment involves more than mere fidelity. Sexual intercourse is most satisfying when it occurs within the security of a total and timeless partnership that is interested in the personal growth of each member.

When two people join to become one in the process of sexual intercourse, a comprehensive unity takes place. To maintain our sexual integrity, we must recognize the facts and implications of a union of this nature. Physical, social, mental, and spiritual dimensions give intercourse a unique significance. However, one must be alert to the danger of so ethereal a view of sexual unity that it does not correspond with the reality of human experience.

The giving of ourselves sexually is symbolic of giving of our personhood. To focus on the level of reproduction or pleasure without considering the deeper significance of communication or unity is to miss the substance of commitment. All four levels are meaningful and important. Yet there is a sequence of intimacy from least to greatest: reproduction, pleasure, communication, and unity. The greater the intimacy the more total is the commitment.

There are many aspects to a total commitment. Strengths and sexuality are merely two of these. Each spouse gives all they are to their mate. This mutual submission is done in a spirit of harmony, sensitivity, friendship, compassion, and humility.

WHAT IS A TIMELESS COMMITMENT?

The wedding vows read, "Till death do us part." That's a terribly long time. How can anyone seriously enter into such a permanent obligation? That's impossible! Far too idealistic. After all, people change, situations change.

- What if you fall out of love?
- What if you don't even like your partner anymore?
- What if somebody more compatible comes along?

Several years ago I went to a seminar on marriage at an international psychological convention. During one of the workshops the question arose: "At what point should one divorce?" The scholarly presenter suggested, "When your needs are no longer met." Someone else added, "When you are unhappy or uncomfortable." The discussion continued with the emphasis that life is too short to waste your time in a relationship that does not bring you pleasure, self-actualization, and ultimate fulfillment.

I was sitting in my chair getting more and more restless and trying hard to bite my tongue. Finally I could hold back no longer and I blurted out, "But what about commitment?"

The room went silent, then people started chuckling. The presenter stepped forward and explained to me, as a father would to a slightly retarded son, "Commitment is an old-fashioned word. Marriage is a social contract and if it no longer meets the needs of the parties involved it must be either renegotiated or nullified."

I shook my head and said in my most intellectual voice, "That's the wimpy way out," but nobody listened.

Relationships go up and down while love comes and goes. Someone once asked Alan Alda, the famous television and movie star, how he managed to have such a long and successful marriage. His answer was that most relationships begin with a "vibrant" love, but soon fade into "utter discontent." It is easy to give up and forget that "love returns in waves...you just have to wait it out."[8] Alan Alda was right; love is like the tides of the ocean. Sometimes they come in and the passion is high. You feel the love and the relationship is wonderful. Then there are times when the tide is out—sometimes way out. The relationship is dry and lifeless. The love is gone. You look out at the sea and wonder if the tide will ever return. But if you're patient and stay at the beach, the waves will again crash on the shore. The excitement and romance will return. You will even feel the love again.

The intent of the marriage commitment is permanence. Yet we live in a culture that sees everything as disposable. If the tide is out at your beach, just go to another. We are impatient and the grass is always greener on the other side of the fence. Robert Fulghum, in his book It Was on Fire When I Lay down on It counters with, "The grass is greenest where it is watered."[9] Unfortunately we don't water our own grass. It is much easier to pick up our things and move. If the relationship does not work out, divorce and try another. Frequently a terminated marriage says more about who we are, than about what was wrong in the relationship.

People trade in marriages the way they trade in cars. A couple in their late twenties came to me for pre-marital counseling. When I confronted her with some potential difficulties in the relationship, she agreed.

"Dr. Stephens, I don't think this marriage has much of a chance to last more than a year."

"Then why are you getting married?"

"He's such a nice guy and I think I should give it a try. If it doesn't work, it just doesn't work."

I was shocked.

Marriage commitments are serious. Two people pledge their integrity to each other. They promise to enjoy the good times and work through the bad. They vow that they will allow nothing to tear apart their union. The future may be unknown, but their honor, determination, and hard work will carry them through.

Tami and I have committed to never use the word *divorce*. Just saying the word opens the option. Threatening it cheapens our integrity. Therefore, we strike the word from our vocabulary. We are both committed to work through any problem and grow deeper in our relationship year by year. This does not guarantee we will always feel wonderful about each other. What it does mean is that our love is more than a feeling, it is a choice.

There is also the realization that it takes two to create marital difficulties. If there is a problem, I ask what it is I have done to either contribute to, or cause the situation. We will work out the problem together.

However, merely staying together does not guarantee a healthy relationship. Many couples proudly announce their commitment for life while they have endured many years of emotional divorce. Years ago I heard a speaker ask the audience what their relationship was like with their spouse, then asked them to determine if they were:

- roommates
- checkmates

- cellmates
- stalemates
- helpmates

The first four options may have a timeless commitment, but it seems as if they are following the letter of the law and ignoring its spirit. The last option, being helpmates, is the heart of a timeless commitment. Two partners helping each other to be their best.

A timeless marriage with timeless growth and intimacy as its aim is a goal that any marriage can achieve if both parties are willing to fight for it.

Earlier in this chapter I said that commitment is based on trust and when trust is broken, the commitment is shattered. Adultery, abandonment, abuse, and addiction destroy the heart of a marriage. The relationship might stay together, but the intimacy is dead. You must circle *cellmates* in the previous paragraph to describe the interaction. A legal divorce is only a technicality.

Yet if the offending party is truly repentant and if the offended can recapture a spark of trust, then it is possible to renew the timeless commitment. This is a difficult thing to do, but when possible, it is well worth reviving the healthy aspects of a relationship.

The dream of growing old together is a wonderful dream. I love to hear of couples celebrating fifty years together—couples who have been true helpmates. At times I have asked them how they do it. The usual answer is, "We have had good times and bad times, but through it all we have been committed to each other."

That is the type of trustworthy, total, and timeless commitment that provides security. It fosters a nurturing environment where two can mature and grow. Anything less is not really a commitment. We live in a world of false vows and counterfeit promises, where people play at marriage. They don't want to be tied down or vulnerable. Halfhearted commitments make marriage a mockery. They doom the partners to superficiality and loneliness.

RENEWING THE COMMITMENT

Commitment is the foundation to any marriage. When it fails, the marriage crumbles. Building a firm marriage gives it the possibility of withstanding anything.

Doug and Diane had made a total and timeless commitment. One evening when Diane was out of town visiting relatives, Doug picked up a prostitute. The next morning he was appalled at what he had done—it was so stupid and terribly wrong. He knew he had to tell Diane, but he was afraid she would leave him.

Diane was shattered. "How could you do this?" she asked, her voice cracking. "I thought you loved me. I thought you were a Christian."

Doug hung his head and cried. "Is there any way you could forgive me?"

A few days later they walked into my office. Doug stuttered through their story as Diane stared at the floor. It was hard for her to look at him and yet she made it clear she didn't want a divorce. Doug was repentant and willing to do anything to reestablish trust. Diane was numb, but she wanted to forgive him and try to rebuild the relationship.

After nine months of intense counseling, these two stood before their minister. It was a sunny June afternoon. She wore her wedding dress and he a tuxedo. Friends and relatives applauded as they renewed their vows to honesty, dependability, and faithfulness. They knelt before God and committed themselves to him. Then they kissed a wild, passionate kiss while the guests cheered and whistled.

I wish the story ended there. A month later Doug applied for life insurance. Part of the routine health exam involved an AIDS test and Doug's results were HIV positive. He couldn't believe it— one night of illicit activity and his life was at risk.

Diane was angry and scared. The two held each other, crying and praying. The next day she went to a community health clinic for anonymous testing. Several days later she found her results were negative, but she should be retested in six months.

Diane moved out to think things through and decide what to do. A week later she returned home with a commitment to stay beside Doug through his terminal crisis. During the next five years her commitment was total.

She went back to the clinic six months later and got a clean bill of health. Together they told friends and relatives of the disease. She went to the doctor with him, encouraged him, and prayed for him. She packed up his personal items when he could no longer work. When he was too exhausted to walk, she pushed him in his wheelchair. She nursed him at home when he could no longer take care of himself.

As the years passed, Doug drastically lost weight, had horrible night sweats, grew large warts on his face, and struggled with his breathing. Before her very eyes, Diane watched Doug slowly die. She was constantly by his side.

Together they went to local churches and high schools, speaking about AIDS and abstinence. Together they committed each day to God and to each other. It wasn't easy and it wasn't romantic. During the last year, Doug was always sick and Diane was always exhausted. She was there by his side, holding his skinny hand and praying the night he died.

The last time I saw Doug and Diane together I asked her why she stayed with him. She smiled and said, "I told him, 'till death do we part,' and I meant it."

"But aren't there times you regret staying with Doug?"

"Not for a minute. During the past few years I've learned that love isn't leaving when things get rough. It's giving and growing through the hard times. I love Doug more now than when we were first married. The bad times taught me what real marriage is all about."

I said, "Most people couldn't do what you've done, but you've shown real commitment in action. Thanks."

Diane blushed and I whispered, "You're quite a lady."

1. James Michener, *Hawaii* (New York: Random House, 1959), 470–486.

2. Howard Gardiner, *Frames of Mind: The Theory of Multiple Intelligences* (New York: Basic Books, Inc., 1983). These strengths are in expanded and modified version of intelligence as presented by Dr. Howard who lists six types of intelligence: linguistic, musical, logical/mathematical, spatial, bodily/kinesthetic, and personal.

3. C. G. Jun, *Memories, Dreams, Reflections* (New York: Vintage, 1989), 173ff.

4. Harry Hollis, *Thank God for Sex* (Nashville: Broadman Press, 1975), 11–12.

5. John 10:10, KJV.

6. Genesis 4:1.

7. Genesis 2:24, KJV.

8. Elizabeth Kay, "Arlene and Alan Alda: A Love Story," *McCall's* (January 1976).

9. Robert Fulghum, *It Was on Fire When I Lay down on It* (New York: Villard Books, 1990), 162.

STRUGGLING

WITH

PARENTING

BRUCE WILKINSON

Bruce Wilkinson
Founder and President of Walk Thru the Bible Ministries
Popular speaker and author

"Do you know who that is?" the man next to me at the conference asked, pointing to a young man on the other side of the auditorium. "That's Rob, the son of that famous Christian leader!" Then he named a man whom I had respected all my life, an internationally known speaker. The first thought that came to my mind was, "I want to talk with him. I'd really like to find out what it was like to grow up in such a godly home as that."

During the next break I made my way over to that young man and introduced myself.

"I'm Bruce Wilkinson," I said, smiling. "I've been an admirer of your father for years. I'd love to know what it was like growing up in your dad's home."

That young man's mouth fell open. He stared at me with cold eyes for a moment, as if trying to get his emotions under control. Finally, he squeezed out, "I hate my father. I hate God." Then he swore a blue streak, muttered, "Stay away from me," and stalked out of the room.

You could have picked my jaw up from off the floor. The son of one of the most famous Christian leaders had just cursed God and said that he hated his father! How on earth could that happen? How did he get to that point? As I pondered this, my thoughts soon turned to my own family. I couldn't think of anything worse than somebody walking up to one of my kids, asking if they were the son or daughter of Bruce Wilkinson, and being sworn at for mentioning my name. My children rejecting the Lord I love and serve? How could I keep that from happening?

After that shattering conversation with the son of the Christian leader, I began to search for an answer to the problem of passing on my faith. My antennae were out, and I was struck over and over again how a downhill slide was apparent in so many areas of life. Churches that began as Gospel-preaching churches began in time to slide toward simply being social gatherings. Colleges that began as places to train men for the ministry began to slide toward liberal academic platforms for anti-God spokesmen. Nearly everywhere I looked in life, even in history, there was an unmistakable downhill slide away from God. That which started in such vibrant faith and resolute commitment, ended generations later in empty faith, continuing conflict, and even atheistic antagonism toward God.

Many churches are birthed as dynamic powerhouses for God, having an impact on their societies in dramatic ways for the redemption of the people and cultures of which they are a part. The Bible is preached openly as the Word of God and every person is seen as in need of eternal salvation. But as times goes on, the wisdom of God becomes less important and the wisdom of man takes preeminence.

I'll never forget more than twenty years ago being invited to speak on a Sunday morning at one of America's most outstanding churches, a body that influenced not only its entire city, but also the whole country. How honored I felt, standing in that pulpit and recounting a bit of their history. But when I said, "Please open your Bibles to the passage of the day," I noticed that no one moved. As I later discovered over lunch, this congregation didn't bother to bring their Bibles to church because the pastor preached more out of *Time* or *Newsweek* than out of *Matthew, Mark, Luke,* or

John. His congregation did not believe even the most basics tenets of the Gospel. For the most part, they were unconverted. They gathered more for the music and social interaction. The entire church had moved from godliness to godlessness.

Years ago on the American Atlantic coast, villages began creating life-saving stations for emergencies at sea. The people would gather for training, prepared in case a ship ran aground. They had life jackets and lifeboats at the ready, and moorage's were soon built so that locals could keep their boats close at hand. Over time, the gathering of people became more important, and the talk of saving lives was less so. Eventually, these gatherings became private clubs which had no interest at all in saving lives. In some cases, those who insisted on saving lives at sea were asked to leave, so that the others could focus on what interested them most—boating and parties. Many of the yacht clubs of the upper Atlantic coast got started just this way. Instead of saving the lives of others, they now focus on meeting their own needs for socializing. That's an apt illustration for many churches today. Founded with the idea of saving lives, they have now rejected the notion of salvation and focus on themselves.

THE THREE GENERATION PRINCIPLE

Scripture reveals the solution to this crucial issue of passing on our faith, and it paves the way for us to understand what things change from one generation to the next. More importantly, the Bible shows us what we can do about it. As you read this chapter, you will begin to understand how we all live in a different "generation." Which one you are in determines a great deal about your life.

Imagine for a moment that you are at a family reunion. Three generations gather together to celebrate the fiftieth wedding anniversary of your parents. Your folks, the oldest generation, have a few health concerns, but no aches or pains are going to dampen this milestone. Married to the same woman for fifty years, your dad still teases his bride as if she were that fifteen-year-old he met on the nearby farm. Next is your generation which has entered middle age. A couple of your siblings have taken to ribbing you because you are nearing forty-eight and the half century mark is only a couple of short years away. The youngest generation is represented by your children, spanning the teen years and early twenties.

The three generations are differentiated not only by age, but by culture and life values. Your generation is very different from your parents' generation, and your children seem to live in a world that is vastly different from yours. When your parents were born in the 1920s, there were no televisions and air travel was nonexistent. Few people had cars, so many never traveled more than a hundred miles from the place of their birth. Library books and an occasional movie were the primary sources for filling up the limited free time. Their lifestyle was harder but not complex.

Your generation brought with it changes, but unlike your children, you weren't raised with shopping malls, computers, or portable phones. Television, opportunities for many to get a college degree, and the space race gave our generation visions of grandeur. You were raised on *I Love Lucy* and *Father Knows Best*, Saturday afternoon baseball, and portable transistor radios.

Now, your children watch *MTV, NYPD Blue,* and *HBO*. They listen to their own CD players, converse with total strangers on the Internet, and spend their free time at shopping malls or playing games on CD-ROM. You wonder, in the quiet moments in late evening, if all this "progress" has been in the right direction. Technology has literally exploded and, though you're not sure, it appears that many people are exploding with it. With the rise of rock 'n' roll came the release of sexual boundaries, and all the liberalizing of morality has degraded culture, destroyed lives with drugs, and demeaned our country's commitment to Christ.

Just yesterday you read on the *USA Today* front page that sixty percent of all couples getting married today will divorce. Sixty percent! Your parents remarked the other day that only one of their friends got divorced. About twenty-five percent of your friends have split. Your children have less than a fifty percent chance of a successful marriage. Is that progress? Or is it a drift away from God? It's different generations, to be sure, and astounding differences economically, physically, socially, morally, and spiritually.

But these are really surface issues, fruit born from hidden roots. In this chapter I want to take the cover off another set of generational differences and reveal what has been going on beneath the surface. The Bible has profound answers to the painful and distressing issue of generational drift. It offers answers for all people, for all time, regardless of when they lived, where they lived, or what they lived for. The Bible even has wisdom for those wondering why they lived in the first place! These generational insights from the pages of Scripture are universal truths. They are supra-cultural, supra-national, and supra-gender. Because the truth is with us all, this truth is for your life, too.

If you are like most of the thousands who have examined these principles, you will feel liberated. It will be like someone walked you out of the murky darkness and brought you into the light. Things that you previously bumped into, that caused confusion and despair, or that frustrated you beyond words, they will now be clear to you. Rarely has anyone heard me present these powerful, transforming truths and had to seek me out later to ask what to do. Once they know the truth, they know exactly what to do.

As you turn these pages and your perceptions grow about yourself and your life, you will become aware that these very same principles govern not only individuals, but all types of organizations. Everything that people are involved with in life is touched by these truths—churches, businesses, even nations. Not only will you know where all of your family and friends fit in the three-part pattern of life, you will know where your church fits, and where your business fits.

THE THREE CHAIRS

In order to make these issues more visual and practical, I have used three different chairs to represent three different generations. Picture them in your mind: the first chair is the one on your left side, the second chair is in the middle, and the third chair sits on the right. By the time you are finished reading this chapter, you will know where you sit, where your parents sit, and where your children sit. Let me introduce you to them now.

As you examine the Bible passages below, you will see that there is movement from *godliness* to *godlessness*. The first chair is our metaphor for the godly person—someone who remains close to Him. The third chair, on the other hand, indicates those who have moved away from God and whose focus is on themselves.

FIRST CHAIR	SECOND CHAIR	THIRD CHAIR
Chair on Left	Chair in Middle	Chair on Right
Joshua 24:1–15 Judges 2:7a, 8–9	Joshua 24:16–31 Judges 1:1–2, 7b	Judges 2:10–23

The First Chair: The Life of Joshua

Joshua is a primary example of a person who sits in the first chair. He knows the Lord and lives his life to serve Him. Every time you see Joshua in the pages of the Bible, you find him seeking to please God in his faith and actions.

Joshua once said to his people, "Now therefore, fear the LORD, serve Him in sincerity and in truth, and put away the gods which your fathers served on the other side of the River and in Egypt. Serve the LORD! *But as for me and my house, we will serve the LORD*" (Joshua 24:14, 15c, NKJV, emphasis added).

Joshua loves the Lord. He has a heart for God. He even commits his family to serving the Lord. Joshua has firsthand faith. This is a man totally devoted to God—the mark of a person in the first chair.

The people of Joshua's generation were also committed to

God. They had seen Him work mighty wonders; they knew God had been with them during the difficult times of taking the land. This generation had firsthand knowledge and experience of the God of the heavens at work in their midst. Again, that's the mark of people in the first chair. They know God firsthand, love Him, and they've seen Him work in their lives. They can pass on the good news of Jesus Christ because they have experienced His mighty power in their own lives.

The Second Chair: The Elders who Outlived Joshua

Let's trace what happened to Joshua's descendants and the generation that outlived him. Read Joshua 24:31 and Judges 2:7b and watch for the two key signs of that second generation:

> Joshua 24:31: "Israel served the LORD all the days of Joshua, and all the days of the elders who outlived Joshua, who had known all the works of the LORD which He had done for Israel."
>
> Judges 2:7: "So the people served the LORD all the days of Joshua, and all the days of the elders who outlived Joshua, who had seen all the great works of the LORD which He had done for Israel."

The child who is raised in a first chair family is most fortunate. He sees with his own eyes the commitment of his parents and how God actually answered the specific prayers of his parents. It was the same in Joshua's day. The second generation received the innumerable benefits of their parents' firsthand faith—they had "known all the works of the LORD which He had done for Israel."

The generation that came after Joshua still believed in the LORD, but there was one significant difference: their faith wasn't original. They hadn't dealt personally with the Lord. Instead, they relied on the faith of their parents and the stories of what God had done in their parents' generation. That alone had been enough to develop faith in God. As children, they either saw the miracles of God's intervention on their parents' behalf, or found out about the Lord's miracles from their fathers and mothers. They heard how God had parted the waters of the Red Sea, brought water from a rock, and provided manna in the wilderness. They believed the stories, but they were a generation removed from actually having dealt with the issue personally. Their parents were the adults who marched around the walls of Jericho, while they themselves only heard about God's miracle in that battle. They believed all the facts about God, but they didn't experience Him personally, that's the second chair.

The Third Chair: Another Generation Arose After Them

You only have to turn a few pages in your Bible to read what happened when the second generation had children. Judges 2:10 tells the sad story: "When all that generation had been gathered to their fathers, another generation arose after them who did not know the LORD nor the work which He had done for Israel."

Do you see it? There are three profound differences between the second and third generations. First, the third generation "did not know the LORD." In other words, they did not know God personally and they were not saved. Tragic, isn't it? The grandchildren of Joshua's day didn't even count themselves as believers.

Second, the third generation "did not know...the work which He (the Lord) had done for Israel." That's difficult to believe, that they didn't even know the stories of the great miracles their grandparents had experienced. They didn't know that the Jericho walls tumbled to the ground because the nation of Israel marched and blew trumpets, or that God parted the Jordan, or that the sun stood still. *They didn't even know about these events.* Why not?

There could be only one reason as I see it: their parents never told them. And why didn't they tell them? Think about it. The moment a father or mother would tell the stories of God's great answers to prayer in their parents' lives, the immediate question in the heart of the child would be, "Where are those great miracles in our lives?" When firsthand faith gets passed on, it always becomes, at that moment, secondhand faith. *And secondhand faith doesn't have any firsthand experiences.* You go through the motions, but there isn't any vibrant reality behind them. Firsthand faith has experienced the reality of God; secondhand faith has only heard about it. By the time we get to thirdhand faith there is no faith left. The people of the third generation don't believe it because there is no reality for them to experience.

The first chair person is saved.
The second chair person is saved.
The third chair person is not saved.
The first chair person has the works of God.
The second chair person has heard about the works of God.
The third chair person doesn't know about the works of God.

What is the result, then, of this thirdhand "unfaith"? Read the next few verses in Judges "Then the children of Israel did evil in the sight of the LORD, and served the Baals; and they forsook the LORD God of their fathers..." (Judges 2:11–12, NKJV).

The person sitting in the third chair *forsakes* the Lord God of their fathers.
The person in the third chair *does evil* in the sight of the Lord.
The person in the third chair *replaces* God with other gods.

No matter where you look in life or in history, this three-stage process holds true. For instance, consider the early days of the founding of America. In the beginning, there were people who had experienced God's miraculous work, and they brought revival to our nation. Followers of Christ believed the hand of God was present in the founding of our nation. The founding documents of our nation are replete with references to our Creator.

The first colleges in this country—Harvard, Princeton,

William and Mary—were all founded to train men to preach the Gospel. They were started by men and women who sat in the first chair; who experienced the providence of God. But, the following generation didn't have the same vital relationship with God, and they carried on those values out of tradition rather than conviction. They continued what the earlier generation had done because "that's the way we've been doing it," not from a resolute commitment to living life so that it was fully pleasing to Jesus Christ. By the time the third generation arrived, any mention of God was a bit of an embarrassment. This third generation has remained in these institutions out of tradition. The Ivy League students of today have told me that even carrying a Bible into a classroom can get you mocked and scorned.

Does that surprise you? It shouldn't, considering the pattern we've just seen in the book of Judges. As the Bible so forthrightly states, the third generation forsakes the God of their fathers, does evil, and serves other gods. What began as a training ground for the people of God has turned into a playroom for those who have rejected God. That's evidence of the generational drift that is at work in our world.

THE THREE CHAIRS IN YOUR LIVING ROOM

Now, let's bring these three chairs into your living room for a moment—because they are there, whether you've seen them or not. If you grew up in a home committed to Jesus Christ, you probably came to know Christ as your personal savior between the ages of five and thirteen. But you may not be nearly as committed to Him and His calling as your parents were, unless you have already paid the price of becoming a first-chair believer. Most Christians today are second-chair believers. They know all about the faith, but it's not vibrant to them. It doesn't significantly shape their values or their lifestyles. They can talk to their children about their walk with God in generational terms, but they have no first-hand experience to pass on.

Unfortunately, those who remain in the second chair typically raise third-chair children. These are the young adults who are leaving the church in untold numbers. Many of these children want no part in the kind of empty faith that they saw in their parents while growing up. In fact, they don't even know that there is such a thing as a first-chair follower of Jesus. They don't see how the Bible affects their lives, and they've got better things to do on Sunday morning than sit in church. So they reject God because they don't know Him.

WHERE DO YOU SIT?

Would you describe yourself as a believer in Jesus who is wholly committed to the Lord? Do you seek to love and serve Him with all your heart? Or would you describe yourself as a believer who has not been able to make Christ the center of his life, filled with uncertainty and internal conflicts about God and the real meaning of life?

Where do you sit? That's the real question. Do you sit in the first chair, experiencing the presence of God and allowing Him to use you, shape you, and minister to others through you? Or do you sit in the second chair, believing the truth and appreciating what God is doing in the lives of others, but always wondering why you don't have the same spiritual passion they do? Look at the overview of where we've gone so far and see if you can find the chair to which you've grown accustomed:

THE FIRST GENERATION	THE SECOND GENERATION	THE THIRD GENERATION
Joshua's Generation	*Elders' Generation*	*Another Generation*
Knows God	Knows God	Knows not God
Has seen the works	Knows about the works	Knows not the works
Serves the Lord	Serves the Lord of fathers	Serves false gods
Firsthand Faith	Secondhand Faith	No Faith

In many ways, the generation you are in determines almost everything in your life: your values, your friends, your goals, and ultimately your destiny. Lets look at some of the characteristics of each generation, and the secret of transitioning to the first chair—and staying there!

RAISING GODLY CHILDREN

I have found that a person's attitude about possessions is one of the best indicators of which chair they are in. A woman in the first chair doesn't really care about the car she drives, as long as it gets her where she wants to go. But one in the second chair wants to arrive in style: "We've got to get a new car," she'll say, "because this one looks pretty tired." She and her husband might discuss that all the way to church, while the kids sit in the back seat taking it all in. Once the family arrives in the church parking lot, everything changes completely. The husband suddenly becomes a junior Billy Graham, gently shaking hands and saying "God bless you" to everyone around. He might even get up in the service to offer a testimony. His children learn early on that a relationship with God extends only to the edge of the church parking lot.

Imagine a dad who offers a long, flowing prayer when company comes over, but who most of the time simply says, "Dear God, thanks for the food. Amen and pass the meat." Imagine a mom who talks in church about the Bible being the most important book in her life, but whose children never see her read it. It doesn't take long for a child to grasp that the church is filled with hypocrites, that everybody is playing games.

Of course, not everyone in the church is playing games. Some people have a dynamic relationship with God, but kids don't know that. The only lives they are really exposed to are the lives of their parents. The only testimonies they hear come from their own second-chair parents who talk only about their conversion because they don't have any other firsthand experiences with God. They have beliefs, but not convictions. You can hold a belief, but a conviction holds you, it dominates you. Beliefs are like opinions, and you can share them with your children, though they may reject them. However, you cannot pass on conviction. Conviction is given by the Holy Spirit to the inner man. Each person must establish a personal relationship with God to really have conviction about Him and His priorities.

COMMANDS AND CONSENSUS

My father is a man of conviction. He sits in the first chair, and has seen God work dramatically to change his life. When my dad speaks to me about his Christianity, I know he has lived his faith. I was one of six kids, and although my dad worked hard to take care of all of us, he took the time regularly to talk with us. Many nights, as I was sitting at our little kitchen table doing my homework, my dad would come in late from work and plop down in the chair across from me so that we could talk. One night I said to him, "Dad, I'm the only guy on the football team who doesn't drink. I want to drink." He looked at me and smiled. "I can understand that," he said.

"No, you can't," I replied. "You never drink. You and Mom have never taken a drink."

"Well, son, that's not really true. Your Mom and I used to drink all the time."

"What?" I was stunned. "You never told me that!"

"Well, you never asked." So he proceeded to tell me some of the details of his earlier life. "If you'd have known us back then, son, you would have seen a big cabinet against the wall, filled with liquor bottles. We drank socially. You know Johnny, who lives up the street? When I first became a Christian, I decided to invite Johnny and his wife over for dinner, so I could share the gospel with them. Mom made a big roast, I poured some good red wine, and we told them we'd just become Christians. The next thing I knew, Johnny was standing in the middle of the room, his hat and coat in hand. 'You call yourselves Christians and you're serving liquor?' he bellowed. Then he grabbed his wife's hand and left the house. Your mother and I looked at each other and decided that if liquor was going to put a barrier between us and non-Christians, we'd get rid of the liquor. That night we poured it all down the drain. I've never had a drink since."

"Wow," I said to him, "but…can I drink sometime? Just to see what it's like?"

"Well, son, that's got to be your choice. You're old enough. But let me ask you a question: Is there a Johnny on your team, watching you?"

As a young man, I got a glimpse into the convictions of a mature Christian. Think about how my father handled that conversation. Had he been sitting in the second chair, our discussion would have been remarkably different.

"Dad, I'm thinking of drinking."

"What?!" he would have replied. "You'd better not ever let me catch you drinking!"

"Why not?"

"Because I said so, that's why not."

"Well, I'm going to do it anyway."

"What will the people at church think if you get caught drinking?"

Of course, this issue has nothing to do with the people at church, but a second-chair person is more interested in what the church will think than in what God will think. A first-chair father has convictions based on the Bible. If the Scripture says to do something, he does it. If it says to refrain from it, he refrains. He is most concerned with the *commands of Scripture*. A second-chair father doesn't think that way. His major concern is with the *consensus of Christians*. The man concerned with the commands of Scripture sets an example of holiness in all areas of his life; the one concerned with the consensus of Christians sets an example of hypocrisy.

The first-chair mother has a *relationship* with God, and it impacts every part of her life. When she sees a need, her first thought is to take it to the Lord in prayer. The second-chair mother has a *responsibility* to God, and that's how she approaches her faith in Christ. She knows she should go to church, and she knows she should donate some time to a ministry, so she fulfills her obligation. But if you follow her around, you'll find out that the only time she talks to God is to say, "Thanks for the food," and that will be only if somebody is watching. If you have a relationship with God, your children will become Christians; if you have a responsibility to God, your kids will get turned off by the demands of "religion."

It seems funny, but it has been my experience that second-chair parents are the ones who are always spouting off Proverbs 22:6: "Train up a child in the way he should go, and when he is old he will not depart from it." Unfortunately, you can't train a child in the way he should go unless you are sitting in the first chair.

CHRIST'S CALL TO CHRISTIANS

Paul warned a group of people in one church that there were some who were spiritual, some who were carnal, and some who were natural or unsaved. That is, in every church there are some people who really know God, some who know about Him, and some who don't know Him at all.

In Revelation 3:15 Christ gives a clarion call to Christians. This is a passage that most people have only a surface understanding of. Christ is speaking to Christians when He says, "I know your deeds, that you are neither cold nor hot. I wish you were one or the other!"

Did you ever stop to ask yourself, "Why?" Why does Jesus want us to be cold or hot? The person sitting in the second chair stands between the first chair and the third, keeping them apart. The guy in the first chair has a message to share with that lost soul in the third chair, but the person in the middle often gets in the way! His weak faith hinders the process of evangelism and it keeps people out of the kingdom. So Jesus says, "Because you are lukewarm—neither hot nor cold—I am about to spit you out of my mouth. You say, 'I am rich; I have acquired wealth and do not need a thing.' But you do not realize that you are wretched, pitiful, poor, blind and naked. I counsel you to buy from me gold refined in the fire, so you can become rich..." (Revelation 3:16–18, NIV).

Jesus is speaking to Christians in this passage. This doesn't mean that He will kick people out of His family; what it means is that their behavior is repugnant to Him. The people in the first chair are wholly committed to God. The next group starts sold out to God but becomes more concerned with possessions, position, prestige, and power. Something else takes the priority rather than God. Jesus warns us, "Those whom I love I rebuke and discipline" (Revelation 3:19a, NIV). He loves us, but He will not stand for our being lukewarm. Christ's call is clear: "Be earnest, and repent. Here I am! I stand at the door and knock. If anyone hears my voice and opens the door, I will come in and eat with him, and he with me" (Revelation 3:19b–20, NIV).

Repentance is getting up off that second chair, confessing your spiritual lukewarmness, and moving over to the first chair. We need to repent of taking God for granted. We often use this passage as an evangelistic message, but the primary message is that Christ is knocking on the hearts of *believers. He wants you to know that it is possible to have a dynamic walk with God. You can move to the first chair!*

In your mind's eye, picture yourself standing up from that second chair and moving with courage and boldness to the first chair. Now visualize yourself sitting down and enjoying the comfort of that chair. You know why it's comfortable? Because it's the Lord's chair, and it's where you belong. It was meant to be yours. You must ask forgiveness and start fresh in your walk with the Lord.

HOW FAMILY LEGACIES ARE CREATED

The principle of the three chairs isn't limited to just families. Nations go through that same process, as do churches, denominations, Bible colleges, and ministries. They start out in the first chair, totally committed to Christ, full of the work of the Holy Spirit. They give way to a "generation" that is sitting in the second chair, that knows Christ and has heard what the Lord has done in the past, but has no personal experience with the works of God. They aren't able to tell what powerful thing God has done in their own lives, so they have little to pass on to the third generation. That generation, the "grandchildren," sit in the third chair, not knowing Christ as Savior. They don't know about the mighty work God has done in the past. They were never told, for fear they would ask the questions, "Why isn't God at work now? How come the Lord doesn't work like that for us?"

The challenge for the church is to get people who are sitting in the second chair to move to the first chair. You see, people who are the sons and daughters of first-chair Christians learn all the truths about God. They generally believe what their parents believe, until they make a break in high school or college and try to determine which part of their faith is their own. As a child you don't know how to think differently from what you have been told. But as you get older you begin to test the beliefs of your parents. Your folks can tell you what they believe, but you want your own experience with God. If you never have an experience with Him, you'll have nothing to pass on to your children. You can teach them the Scriptures, and you can tell them the lessons, but wisdom comes from experience.

For example, many of us grew up in homes where the family had devotions together every day. But once we left home, we never practiced daily devotions. Do you know why that is? *Because we weren't having devotions; our parents were having them for us.* Our parents had a conviction about the importance of daily time in the Word, but we never developed that conviction for ourselves.

That's why the second generation is where the cause of Christ is either won or lost. They will either decide to move to the first chair and experience total commitment to Christ, or they will remain in the second chair and allow their faith to wither away.

THE CHAIR OF BONDAGE

Nobody sits in the first chair all the time. Most of us would say that it's our desire to be there most of the time, but the fact is that we have a tendency to slide over to the second chair. Ambition, possessions, and power creep into our lives, and pretty soon we're thinking more about ourselves than about God, and we've plopped down into the second chair without realizing it. John tells us that those worldly things get in the way—the lust of the flesh, the lust of the eyes, and the pride of life. But he also warns us that these things come "not from the Father but from the world" (1 John 2:16, NIV). When you turn your attention to those worldly things, you compromise your convictions as a first-chair person.

Too many people have bought into the world's concept of "success." I often talk with working mothers who claim they "have to work" if they are going to pay their bills. But when you look at the bills, you often see that they represent the values of this materialistic culture. They want to have a nice home, so they spend their time at work rather than with their children. They want nice cars, nice furniture, and nice clothes for everyone, so they "have to work to meet the needs." It's an argument based on a lie. In actuality, truth is that unless both parents work they cannot live according to their *wants.* Though God has promised to provide for our needs, they choose not to be content with that.

The second chair is a chair of bondage. It binds people into a selfish lifestyle. It keeps them bound up through debt, mortgages, and a constant desire for *more.* We all know what that feels like. Let's say your station wagon is getting a little tired. It uses a bit of oil, there are stains on the seat, and the style is a bit outdated.

What you really want is a minivan, with a bit more room and a more modern appearance. You dream about it, plan for it, and finally the day comes when you actually take possession of a new minivan, and you feel fulfilled...for a while. Then one day somebody at the mall opens his door into it and leaves a dent. The kids spill grape soda on the carpet. The water pump breaks and it has to go in for repairs. It isn't very long and your minivan isn't making you feel fulfilled any more. So you have to go get something else to return that feeling of satisfaction to your life. And the cycle starts all over again.

Our culture is based on consumption. We are deluged with advertising that tells us we aren't complete in some way, and that the product being offered is the one that will complete us. Our teeth aren't white enough, our hair isn't bouncy enough, and our automobiles aren't classy enough, so we need to buy a new product that will fill that "need." Our society is based on this kind of thinking, and people in the second chair have become part of its system. It's a chair of bondage.

THE CHAIR OF SUBMISSION

God's Word warns us that "the world and its desires pass away, but the man who does the will of God lives forever" (1 John 2:17, NIV). Too many Christians spend all their time dreaming, scheming, and steaming over temporal things, things that won't last. John reminds us that it is eternal things that are to be on the hearts and minds of God's people. Rather than worrying about what the *world* wants, we ought to be concerned with what God wants. That's why James reminds us that "friendship with the world is hatred toward God" (James 4:4, NIV), and Paul exhorts us to "be not conformed to the pattern of this world, but be transformed by the renewing of your mind" (Romans 12:2).

Though we live in it, Christians are not part of this world or its system. If Satan is the "god of this world" (2 Corinthians 4:4), we ought to reject the system and turn to the one true God. Jesus, in the Sermon on the Mount, encourages people not to focus on the riches of this world: "Do not store up for yourselves treasures on earth, where moth and rust destroy, and where thieves break in and steal. But store up for yourselves treasures in heaven, where moth and rust do not destroy, and where thieves do not break in and steal. For where your treasure is, there your heart will be also" (Matthew 6:19–21, NIV). Christ knew that your earthly investments reveal your heavenly commitments. Those who sit in the second chair have hearts that are concerned with the people of this world and with the will of God.

The first chair is a chair of submission. The people who sit in it submit to the will of God, *even though they know they will be ostracized from the world* because the world doesn't understand God or His ways. In fact, the world hates God, which is why it killed His Son. And "if the world hates you, keep in mind that it hated me first," the Lord said to His disciples in the upper room on the day He was crucified. "If you belonged to the world, it would love you as its own. As it is, you do not belong to the world, but I have chosen you out of the world. That is why the world hates you" (John 15:18–19, NIV).

Have you ever considered yourself hated by this world? Christ Himself said that when you represent Him, that's what happens. Christians in the first chair submit themselves to God, regardless of the outcome in this world.

Those who sit in the second chair don't want to be hated by the world. They want to be loved by the world, and they do all sorts of things to compromise so that they'll be accepted. God's priorities are not their priorities, and when their children see them talking about the right things but living the wrong values, those children live in conflict.

If you sit in the first chair, you see Scripture as the only truth. The Bible guides your life and your actions. But if you spend much of your life in the second chair, you begin to see the Bible as being quaint or dated. You ignore passages that are inconvenient to your lifestyle. For example, much of the Christian community in our culture is being subverted by television. On TV, everything having to do with God is mocked and criticized. Immorality and sexual innuendo is everywhere. Yet the average Christian adult in this country watches thirty-two hours of television per week (and claims to be too busy to take a position of service in the church). You see, the second chair is full of compromise, but the first chair is full of obedience to God.

THE REBUKE OF GOD

It's time for Christians in our culture to wake up to the fact that we are sliding down a long, slippery slope of compromise. We live in a culture with an embarrassment of riches, and we think that we are pretty well-off. We think we are rich because we have acquired so many possessions, but Jesus says to us, "You say, 'I am rich; I have acquired wealth and do not need a thing.' But you do not realize that you are wretched, pitiful, poor, blind and naked" (Revelation 3:17, NIV).

Some people have mistaken material wealth for the blessing of God. They think that earthly riches are a sign of God's pleasure with us. What nonsense! Didn't Jesus say, after meeting the rich young ruler, that it is easier for a camel to go through the eye of a needle than for a rich man to enter the kingdom of God? The rich reject God because they don't feel their need for Him, or because they aren't willing to surrender all to the Almighty. Now, if it is difficult for a rich man to get into heaven, then most of us in modern day America are going to have a really tough time. We live in one of the wealthiest of times ever. The average American's income ranks in the top five percent of the world's economy. We have so many possessions that we have had to start an entirely new industry, the self-storage structure, simply to contain all our extra stuff. The average American homeowner can't fit his belongings into his personal dwelling—and that's probably unprecedented in world history.

So when Jesus warns of the difficulties for the rich to get into heaven, He's talking about us. He is rebuking us, and warning us of our lifestyle. "No one can serve two masters. Either he will hate the one and love the other, or he will be devoted to the one and despise the other. You cannot serve both God and Money" (Matthew 6:24, NIV). The love for money and the desire for popularity with the world are the two great motivators for people in the second chair. But the choices we make on this earth have eternal consequences.

Jesus Christ demands action. If you are going to choose to leave a godly legacy, your values will have to be revealed in your actions so that your children can see your commitment to Christ, not just hear about it. Your life's influence on your kids will imprint them forever. What heritage do you want to pass on?

CREATING A GODLY LEGACY

We are called as Christian parents to leave a godly legacy. Moses emphasized how important it is to the family that the parents love God:

> Hear, O Israel: The LORD our God, the LORD is one. Love the LORD your God with all your heart and with all your soul and with all your strength. These commandments that I give you today are to be upon your hearts. Impress them on your children. Talk about them when you sit at home and when you walk along the road, when you lie down and when you get up. Tie them as symbols on your hands and bind them on your foreheads. Write them on the doorframes of your houses and on your gates. (Deuteronomy 6:4–9, NIV)

If you want to leave a legacy, *love God.* Make your love for Him visible. Talk about the Lord with your kids. Take a stand for God in a culture that hates holiness. Sit in the first chair and experience the life-changing power of the Lord in your life, and you will set an example for them to follow. If you stay in the second chair and merely tell your kids about what God *could* do, you don't give them a chance to actually see God at work.

I have had parents tell me, "I trained up my child in the way he should go, and God isn't keeping His promise!" I often wonder if those parents have a vital *relationship* with God, or if they simply have accepted the *religion* surrounding Him. You see, when you sit in the first chair, you become emotionally passionate about God.

Half of all Christian marriages are in serious trouble these days. These difficulties have an impact on the children in these families and cast a shadow over their legacy. Most of these troubled marriages will eventually produce troubled children. The reason behind the trouble, I think, is that the parents are sitting in the wrong chair. If you take a seat in the second chair, you'll develop problems because you are not living a life of integrity. Your marriage will develop problems. Eventually, your family will, too.

If you really want to overcome those troubles, you need to become a first-chair believer, putting Jesus first. Let Him unleash His power and change your life. Your spouse will see it, and your relationship will change. Your children will see it, and they'll be changed. You *can* leave a godly legacy by establishing Jesus Christ as the center of your life, and letting Him change the way you live.

But be warned: it won't always be easy. He calls you to service. He calls you to commitment. He might call you to significantly change your lifestyle. But as your children see you change, as they see something significant and eternal take hold of your life, they will begin to understand the reality of God, and want Him in their own lives. When they do, your godly legacy will be established.

Moses is an example of one who sat in the first chair—loving and serving God as he led the nation of Israel. When Moses grew old, he left his country in the hands of Joshua, who also had a vibrant relationship with God. Joshua experienced the power of the Lord throughout his life, and credited his many victories to

God's intervention. When Joshua's life drew to a close, he too wanted to ensure that his country would always remember and revere the Lord. He gathered all the people together, and he reminded them that, though their ancestors had been pagans, God had chosen the Jews to bless all nations and had accomplished great things on their behalf. Joshua exhorted everyone to remain true to the Lord. "But if serving the LORD seems undesirable to you, then choose for yourselves this day whom you will serve, whether the gods your forefathers served beyond the River, or the gods of the Amorites, in whose land you are living. But as for me and my household, we will serve the LORD" (Joshua 24:15, NIV). Joshua knew who the King is. He knew the importance of remaining faithful to God, and of sitting in the first chair with the heavenly Father.

There is no passage in Scripture where God says, "Try to obey me." God is interested in results, not just intentions. He instructs us to reach all nations, and He expects us to do just that. He instructs us to raise godly kids, and He won't be satisfied with having us respond, "Well, Lord, we gave it a try." You can't be a first-chair person unless you commit to developing first-chair children. If you don't disciple your children toward godliness, you will "inoculate" them against the things of the Spirit.

In the medical field, inoculation is when the doctor gives you enough of the germs, usually the flu, to help your body build up a resistance to the disease. That keeps you from getting sick when the flu season hits. Christian parents can spiritually inoculate their children against the things of God by giving them just enough of the rules and regulations without sharing the joy and vibrancy of the Holy Spirit. The children learn that God is real but church is boring and Christianity is a series of rules to follow. They become resistant to the things of God, and they wind up spending their lives in the second or third chair.

Raising godly children is your responsibility, Christian parent. You cannot delegate it to the youth pastor, to the Sunday school teacher, or even to God Himself. He gave them to *you*, and He's going to hold you responsible. There is no blaming the world, the television, the school, or the peer group for failures. Those are all significant circumstances, but they don't change the command of God to parents.

Many people seem to think it's impossible to raise godly kids in this age, but I don't buy that. Our society isn't the most godless the world has ever seen, and there are plenty of parents successfully raising godly children in spite of the culture. It's their responsibility. Granted, it's a tough job. I think it's the toughest task anyone can take on, and it seems to foster a feeling of failure in many. I don't feel competent to do it all of the time, but the Lord hasn't instructed me to feel competent. He's just ordered me to do it. I make mistakes, but the fact remains that the one thing I want to accomplish in my family is leaving a godly legacy.

Now, what are some of the ways we can do that?

PRAY WITH YOUR CHILDREN

Late one night, my son and I took a walk together. We were talking about things that were important to us, and praying as we walked. At that time we had a young woman who was pregnant living with us, whom we were trying to help. As our prayers turned toward that young lady's troubles, my son suddenly said, "You know, Dad, she's not saved."

"I know," I replied, looking at my watch. It was getting late, almost 11 P.M.

"What if we were to pray that she trusts Christ tonight?" he asked me.

"I think that's a good idea, son."

"Do you think she'll still be up?"

"Well," I replied, "She's pretty tired. I doubt it." Then I looked at my boy and asked, "What do you want to do?"

"I think we should pray and ask God to keep her up, so that we can talk to her."

So we prayed for that very thing as we walked the rest of the way home. I made sure he was the one to ask, because I wanted him to know what it's like to sit in the first chair. He said something like, "Lord, keep her up. Help her to trust Christ when we get home tonight." Meanwhile, I was praying silently, asking the Lord to use this opportunity to build the faith of my boy. As we walked through the door of our home, the young lady was standing in the living room. "I don't know what's wrong," she said to us. "I just can't get to sleep."

My son looked at me and smiled. And she gave her heart to Jesus that very night.

Have you ever noticed how Christian parents are sometimes afraid to pray for big things with their children? They'll pray for "safe" things, things they know will probably happen whether they pray or not.

"Give Grandpa a safe trip."

"Help Suzy get over her cold."

"Take care of all of us."

And of course there's nothing *wrong* with praying for those things. We are encouraged in Scripture to pray at all times, on all occasions, with all kinds of requests. But it doesn't take much faith to pray for things that we know will probably turn out all right, and it does little for building the faith of our children. I think the reason behind this sort of praying is that parents are worried that the faith of their kids will be shattered if they pray for something great and it doesn't come to pass. But if we don't believe in a God who has the power to do great things, why bother praying at all? If God can't supernaturally work in a situation, what are we doing wasting our time in church on Sundays? We could be home catching all the games on television!

But we *do* have a supernatural, prayer-answering God. He knows what we need, and He is waiting for us to ask Him to work in our lives. My editor, Dr. Chip MacGregor, told me a story about praying with his three-year-old son when they went to pick up

Mrs. MacGregor at a big conference center. Pulling into a taxi zone, Chip realized he only had a few minutes to find his wife in the vast crowd.

His young son, recognizing the problem, said, "Well, why don't we pray?" Then he folded his little hands and said, "Dear Jesus, help us find Mommy right away!" As he looked up, the crowd seemed to part and his mother came walking straight toward them.

"It worked!" the boy cried. "God answered my prayer!"

Faith is built from these kinds of situations. It wasn't the father who received the answer to prayer, but the son. Prayer will help your children experience first-chair things.

Asaph, the psalmist, said to his people:

O my people, hear my teaching; listen to the words of my mouth. I will open my mouth in parables, I will utter hidden things from of old—what we have heard and known, what our fathers have told us. *We will not hide them from their children; we will tell the next generation the praiseworthy deeds of the LORD, his power, and the wonders he has done.* (Psalm 78:1–4, NIV, emphasis added)

Remember, the people in the first chair experience the works of God for themselves. The people in the second chair don't, but they know about the works. The people in the third chair don't even know about the works of the Lord. It is your responsibility to share His works with your children in such a way that they have their own experiences. Pray with them for God to do great things. Tell them about the answers to prayer you have seen recently. Your example will lead them to a first-chair experience of their own.

TELL YOUR CHILDREN THE STORIES OF GOD

It is God's will that you teach the Bible to your kids. To fail to do so is disobedience. You've got to get into the habit of storytelling with your children, so that they know what God has done in the past.

Children love stories. Stories take a complex world and turn it into bite-sized chunks. Kids come to understand the world through stories. That's why little ones will want to hear the same story time after time. When my children were little, I'd read a favorite book to them. As soon as I got to the end and closed the book, they'd reach over and open it to the beginning again, expecting me to repeat the story immediately. Parents might get sick of hearing the same old story again and again, but that's how children learn.

If you want your children to learn about God, *tell them the stories of God.* Do you remember all those great Old Testament stories you learned in Sunday school? Teach them to your children, over and over. The parables of Jesus? Let your kids hear them. The stories about Jesus' life? Repeat them again and again so that your kids understand the uniqueness of Christ.

Asaph had more to say in Psalm 78:

> He decreed statutes for Jacob and established the law in Israel, which he *commanded our forefathers to teach their children,* so the next generation would know them, even the children yet to be born, and they in turn would tell their children. Then they would put their trust in God and would not forget his deeds but would keep his commands. (Psalm 78:5–7, NIV)

Too many Americans have stopped the ritual of storytelling. Families used to keep their stories alive so that the younger generations knew what it was like for the ancestors "back in the old country." Many families told of being related to famous Americans, fighting in the Civil War, or going through Ellis Island when they immigrated. We've stopped doing that, maybe because we have no regard for the past or maybe just because we take it all for granted. But we ought to be telling the stories, especially the stories of God, until the kids cry out, "Wait! Let *me* tell it this time!" When they hear it enough times, they'll be able to relate it to their own kids, and the legacy can be passed on to another generation.

Asaph's point is that if you tell your children the stories of God they will put their trust in God. According to John, God's words are written specifically so that we will believe that Jesus is the Christ, the Son of God. Tell your children the stories of God's Word, and trust that it will have that affect on them.

People who sit in the first chair are familiar with God's Word. Let your kids see you reading it. Make sure they hear you and your spouse talking about it, so that they know you use Scripture as part of your regular interaction with others. Let them know you're thinking about the things of God. When they see how highly you value God's perspective on life as expressed in the Bible, they will value its wisdom too. But they must see you interacting with Scripture. If they hear you *talk about* reading the Bible, but never see you *do* it, they'll figure it's just another good intention, like not watching too much television or limiting yourself to one piece of pie. There's a big difference between a good intention and actual obedience. If you want to raise godly children, read your Bible. It's like putting them in your lap as you sit in the first chair. They can see how important and powerful God's Word is to you, and they'll want that for themselves.

SET A GODLY EXAMPLE FOR YOUR CHILDREN

Let's face it: if you really want to raise godly kids, you're going to have to lead a godly life. You can't fake a spiritual life and have that example somehow blossom into real holiness in the lives of your children. Parenting is hard work, so you might as well decide now whether or not you're serious about your walk with Christ. Moses tells us in Deuteronomy 4:9 to "be careful, and watch yourselves closely so that you do not forget the things your eyes have seen or let them slip from your heart as long as you live."

That's the core issue of being a first-chair parent: if you keep yourself close to God, you'll try to nurture your children's relationship with Him. If you're in the second chair, you don't have much to say to your kids about God. You don't really know the thoughts of God, since you only read the Bible when you have to. You have nothing to pass on as your legacy.

Moses goes on to say that we need to tell our children about what we have seen, "Teach them to your children and to their children after them" (Deuteronomy 4:9b, NIV). It's your job to help your children understand God, and you can't teach what you don't know. Moreover, it's your job to help your *grandchildren* know God.

My kids have terrific grandparents. My folks take our kids away for a long weekend once a year. We call it "grandparents' weekend," and we've been doing it for years. Everyone who attends has to lead a devotional. They spend their time talking about the faith. They discuss what it means to be a Wilkinson. What do we believe? What do we stand for? They tell family stories, so the kids get a sense of history. I think it's one of the most important things that happens each year.

Moses reminds the people of Israel, "Remember the day you stood before the LORD your God at Horeb, when He said to me, 'Assemble the people before me to hear my words so that they may learn to revere me as long as they live in the land and may teach them to their children'" (Deuteronomy 4:10, NIV). In other words, tell your children how you became a Christian. Tell them of your significant spiritual experiences. Keep track of answered prayers, and rejoice over them as a family. As they get older, show them how you read Scripture, and what you do in your prayer closet. Talk about the things you are learning from the Bible. Let them see that Christianity isn't just what happens on Sunday mornings, but it is a constant relationship between you and the Lord Jesus Christ. Then they'll know what it's like to sit in the first chair and they won't be satisfied with a second-chair existence.

TALK TO YOUR CHILDREN
ABOUT SPIRITUAL THINGS

I love the Lord Jesus Christ. He is present with me at all times, and I want my life to reflect Him. Jesus is part of my conversation with others. His name often comes up. Jesus is also part of my thought process, and before making decisions I spend time with Him. A first-chair person tries to be in constant communication with the Savior.

As a parent, my goal is to reveal my relationship with Christ to my children so that they can establish a similar relationship. Deuteronomy Chapter 6, a passage we have already looked at, offers four principles on how to do that:

> Love the LORD your God with all your heart and with all your soul and with all your strength. These command-ments that I give you today are to be upon your hearts. Impress them on your children. Talk about them when you sit at home and when you walk along the road, when you lie down and when you get up. Tie them as symbols on your hands and bind them on your foreheads. Write them on the doorframes of your houses and on your gates. (Deuteronomy 6:5–9, NIV)

The first principle is that I need to impress the truth of God on my kids. That is, I need to teach them about God from the Bible and my own experience. The word "impress," used in this passage was often also used in reference to making pottery. When the clay was still soft, the potter could use a sharp tool to make impressions on his work of art. He might carve a fancy design, or press pieces of colorful stone into the clay. Then, as the clay aged, it became hard and permanently took on the impressions the pot-ter had made. Our children are like clay. We are to impress upon them the truth of God while they are still young. Then as they grow up, those impressions will remain a part of their lives. As you talk to your children, impress them with the truth of God.

The second thing this passage suggests is that *I need to talk with them at various times about God.* Find various times in the day to work your love of God into the conversation. Talk about Him when you get up in the morning, and when you go to bed. Let God be part of your conversation when you share a meal, when you're traveling in the car, and when you're just sitting around the house. This doesn't mean that you need to turn every event of your life into an object lesson. Moses isn't suggesting that you ladle on the spiritual truth in some sort of artificial manner. He is saying that those who sit in the first chair make God part of their normal conversation, and we are to include our kids in it. If He has blessed you, tell your family. If He has revealed something to you during your quiet time, talk to your kids about it. If there is a godly principle that speaks to the moment at hand, use it as you discuss the situation. Make God part of your discussions about what videos to watch and which books to read. If God is Lord of all your life, there is no limit to the way you can talk about Him.

Moses points out that we should be talking and teaching our kids all the time, and that requires a bit of planning. I encourage parents to figure out what they need to be working on with their kids. What are the areas in which your children need to grow? Plan to talk about those things in the normal course of conversation.

Remember, you are parenting all the time. When I was a young man I didn't understand that. I figured my time at home was *my* time. But I matured and realized that I was being selfish and neglecting my responsibility. When I leave the office I am no longer CEO of an organization. When I step in the door of my home, I take on the role of father. I spend my time at home raising godly kids. It's funny, but between work, parenting, fostering my relationship with my wife, and my own spiritual growth, there isn't much time left for anything else! But that's how it's going to be if you want to fulfill the biblical responsibility of being a parent. You have to die to self. Your flesh is tired and wants to relax, and you feel that you deserve it. But if you get into the habit of "zoning out," you'll find you aren't doing your job as a parent. Sure, everybody needs a little time away, and I encourage you to plan some into your schedule so that you can get your batteries recharged every now and again. But *your* needs will take second place to the needs of your kids.

Talk to your children. Many parents never really communicate with their kids, and it causes all kinds of problems when their little kids become teens. Suddenly there's rebellion and a total lack of communication. *So turn off the television and talk.* Agree to shut it off for a month and see what happens. Or limit TV watching to weekends only, and see if you don't converse more as a family.

Parents usually want to talk at mealtimes, because the entire family is together. But kids are more prone to talk at bedtime when it's just the two of you. So turn off the TV, go sit on their bed, and talk. Show them you're committed to communicating with them. You don't have to say much, just ask them about their day and let them share what's going on in their lives. You'll find out what they need and what struggles they are facing. They are your kids and they need to learn from you.

The third thing Deuteronomy 6 tells us is that *I need to display my faith to my children.* Moses spoke of "binding signs to the forehead," which was an Old Testament method for showing what you believed in. The Jews would actually put Scripture passages in a small box and tie it around their heads so that it rested on the forehead. When you saw them, you knew what they stood for. The idea is to show your children that you aren't afraid to be recognized as a Christian. Maybe there's a bumper sticker on your car, or a pin in your lapel, or a logo on your business card that identifies you as a Christian. Perhaps you marched in the pro-life rally or wrote a letter to the editor that took a stand for Christian values. Let your children know that you are proud to be identified with Christ.

Once, when my family went to a restaurant, my daughter, Jenny, suddenly pointed to another family.

"Dad! Look at those people over there!"

I looked over to see a woman who sat alone with five kids, their heads bowed in prayer. "What about them?"

"I've never seen anybody pray in a restaurant besides us!" she replied.

Sometimes young people can feel out of place, that it's "weird" to be Christians in an un-Christian world. Help them to understand that you're proud to be a Christian, and that you *want* to be identified with Christ. Later they'll understand that God's people have always been persecuted, because this world hates God. But that means we're identifying ourselves with Jesus Christ. The world hated Him, too.

What do people see when they watch you? First-chair Christians aren't afraid to be identified with Christ, even though it's out of place with the world.

The fourth principle in that passage from Deuteronomy is that *I am to make my home honoring to God.* Moses talks about writing God's truth on the doors and gates of our homes. Think about it: when people look around your home, what do they see? What books do they see on your shelves? What movies are sitting beside the VCR? What's playing on the radio? Can people who enter there sense they are in a Christian home? Make your house a temple for the Lord. Create an environment that fosters spiritual development. This makes talking about spiritual things easier and more natural in your family.

NEVER GIVE UP ON YOUR CHILDREN

As a parent, your responsibility doesn't end when your children turn eighteen. They're your kids forever, and God says they remain your legacy. Not long ago I was talking with a man whose daughter had an affair, left her spouse, and filed for divorce. He was just torn up about it, but I'll tell you what that brother did. He went to work. He and his wife flew down to meet with her. They got her involved with other relatives. They counseled her, and eventually they brought about a restoration in the marriage. I have deep respect for that man, because in most cases in our culture, the parents would simply have shaken their heads and sadly watched the events proceed. Your children remain yours forever—don't give up on them. Just because they reach eighteen, or move out of the house, doesn't mean you stop parenting.

I think that's the real message of Deuteronomy Chapter 6. It offers us help with the nitty-gritty of Christian parenting: "These are the commands, decrees and laws the LORD your God directed me to teach you to observe in the land that you are crossing the Jordan to possess, so that you, your children and their children after them may fear the LORD your God as long as you live by keeping all his decrees and commands that I give you, and so that you may enjoy long life" (Deuteronomy 6:1–2, NIV).

All of time is linked together in God's mind; He sees the entire scene from beginning to end and into eternity. The reason He waits to judge mankind is that the impact of our lives does not cease when we die. He waits until the full influence of every person, for good or evil, is complete. Parents will be judged—it's their responsibility to raise godly children. Did we help our children understand the Lord? Did we tell them the stories of God? Did we set a godly example before them, so that they know what a mature Christian is? Godly parents are the key to godly children.

I'm constantly amazed at people who sit in the second chair and wonder why their kids don't love God. Some of them have devotions with their kids, some even send them to Christian schools, but they've never figured out that their personal example outweighs any other factor. Do you love the Lord with all your heart, soul, mind, and strength? First-chair people do. And they continue to set that example, no matter how old their children are.

Are you leaving a legacy of godly children? If you want to see your kids choose to sit in the first chair, help them experience first-chair things. Pray with them. Take them on activities with you so they can see how a mature Christian behaves. Develop a ministry that you and your kids can do together. Ask them to give a testimony. Encourage them by putting them in leadership positions. Have them help you when you're asked to serve. Send them on mission trips, which is perhaps the most significant spiritual tool God uses with young people. All of these things reveal the first-chair life to them. And that will cause them to become a godly legacy, which is the goal of Christian parenting.

Struggling

with

Money

JOHN PIPER

John Piper
Pastor of Bethlehem Baptist Church
Author and conference speaker

Money is the currency of Christian Hedonism. What you do with it—or desire to do with it—can make or break your happiness forever. The Bible makes clear that what you feel about money can destroy you:

> Those who desire to be rich fall into temptation, into a snare, into many senseless and hurtful desires that plunge men into ruin and destruction. (1 Timothy 6:9)

Or what you do with your money can secure the foundation of eternal life:

> They are to be liberal and generous, thus laying up for themselves a good foundation for the future, so that they may take hold of the life which is life indeed. (1 Timothy 6:18, 19)

These verses teach us to use our money in a way that will bring us the greatest and longest gain. That is, they advocate Christian

Hedonism. They confirm that it is not only permitted but commanded by God that we flee from destruction and pursue our full and lasting pleasure. They imply that all the evils in the world come not because our desires for happiness are too strong, but because they are so weak that we settle for fleeting pleasures that do not satisfy our deepest souls, but in the end destroy them. The root of all evil is that we are the kind of people who settle for the love of money instead of the love of God (1 Timothy 6:10).

BEWARE THE DESIRE TO BE RICH

This text in 1 Timothy 6 is so crucial that we should meditate on it in more detail. Paul is warning Timothy against

> (5)…men who are depraved in mind and bereft of the truth, imagining that godliness is a means of gain. (6) There is great gain in godliness with contentment; (7) for we brought nothing into the world, and we cannot take anything out of the world; (8) but if we have food and clothing, with these we shall be content. (9) But those who desire to be rich fall into temptation, into a snare, into many senseless and hurtful desires that plunge men into ruin and destruction. (10) For the love of money is the room of all evils; it is through this craving that some have wandered away from the faith and pierced their hearts with many pangs.

Paul writes to Timothy a word of warning about slick deceivers who discovered they could cash in on the upsurge of godliness in Ephesus. According to verse five, these puffed-up controversialists treat godliness as a means of gain. They are so addicted to the love of money that truth occupies a very subordinate place in their affections. They don't "rejoice in the truth." They rejoice in tax evasion. They are willing to use any new popular interest to make a few bucks.

Nothing is sacred. If the bottom line is big and black, the advertising strategies are a matter of indifference. If godliness is in, then sell godliness. This text is very timely. Ours are good days for profits in godliness. The godliness market is hot for booksellers and music makers and dispensers of silver crosses and fish buckles and olive-wood letter-openers and bumper stickers and lucky-water crosses with Jesus on the front and miracle water inside guaranteed to make you win at Bingo or your money back in ninety days. These are good days for gain in godliness!

In his day or in ours, Paul could have responded to this effort to turn godliness into gain by saying, "Christians don't live for gain. Christians do what's right for its own sake. Christians aren't motivated by profit." But that's *not* what Paul said. He said (in verse six), "There is great gain in godliness with contentment."

Instead of saying Christians don't live for gain, he says Christians ought to live for greater gain than the slick money lovers do. Godliness is the way to get this great gain, but only if we are content with simplicity rather than greedy for riches. "Godliness *with contentment* is great gain."

If your godliness has freed you from the desire to be rich and has helped you be content with what you have, then your godliness is tremendously profitable. "For while physical training is a little profitable, godliness is profitable for all things, as it holds promise for the present life and also for the life to come" (1 Timothy 4:8). Godliness that overcomes the craving for material wealth produces great spiritual wealth. The point of verse six is that it is very profitable not to pursue wealth.

What follows in verses 7–10 are three reasons why we should not pursue riches.

But first let me insert a clarification. We live in a society in which many legitimate businesses depend on large concentrations of capital. You can't build a new manufacturing plant without millions of dollars in equity. Therefore, financial officers in big businesses often have the responsibility to build reserves, for example, by selling shares to the community. When the Bible condemns the desire to get rich, it is not necessarily condemning a business which aims to expand and therefore seeks larger capital reserves. The officers of the business may be greedy for more personal wealth, or they may have larger, nobler motives of how their expanded productivity will benefit people.

Even when a competent person in business is offered a raise or a higher paying job and accepts it, that is not enough to condemn him for the desire to be rich. He may have accepted the job because he craves the power and status and luxuries the money could bring. Or, content with what he has, he may intend to use the extra money for founding an adoption agency or giving a scholarship or sending a missionary or funding an inner-city ministry.

Working to earn money for the cause of Christ is not the same as desiring to be rich. What Paul is warning against is not the desire to earn money to meet our needs and the needs of others; he is warning against the desire to *have* more and more money and the ego boost and material luxuries it can provide.

Let's look at the three reasons Paul gives in verses 7–10 for why we should not aspire to be rich.

(1) In verse seven he says, "For we brought nothing into the world and we cannot take anything out of the world." There are no U-Hauls behind hearses.

Suppose someone passes empty-handed through the turnstiles at a big city art museum and begins to take the pictures off the wall and carry them importantly under arm. You come up to him and say, "What are you doing?"

He answers, "I'm becoming an art collector."

"But they're not really yours," you say, "and besides, they won't let you take any of those out of here. You'll have to go out just like you came in."

But he answers again, "Sure, they're mine. I've got them under my arm. People in the halls look at me as an important dealer.

And I don't bother myself with thoughts about leaving. Don't be a kill-joy."

We would call this man a fool! He is out of touch with reality. So is the person who spends himself to get rich in this life. We will go out just the way we came in.

Or picture 269 people entering eternity in a plane crash in the Sea of Japan. Before the crash there is a noted politician, a millionaire corporate executive, a playboy and his playmate, a missionary kid on the way back from visiting grandparents.

After the crash they stand before God utterly stripped of Master-Cards, checkbooks, credit lines, image clothes, how-to-succeed books, and Hilton reservations. Here are the politician, the executive, the playboy, and the missionary kid, all on level ground with nothing, absolutely nothing in their hands, possessing only what they brought in their hearts. How absurd and tragic the lover of money will seem on that day—like a man who spends his whole life collecting train tickets and in the end is so weighed down by the collection he misses the last train. Don't spend your precious life trying to get rich, Paul says, "for we brought nothing into the world and we can take nothing out of the world."

(2) Then in verse 8 Paul adds the second reason not to pursue wealth: "If we have food and clothing, with these we shall be content." Christians can be and ought to be content with the simple necessities of life.

I'll mention three reasons why such simplicity is possible and good.

First, when you have God near you and for you, you don't need extra money or extra things to give you peace and security.

> Keep your life free from the love of money. Be content with what you have. For he has said, "I will never fail you nor forsake you." Hence we can confidently say, "The Lord is my helper, I will not be afraid; what can man do to me?" (Hebrews 13:5–6)

No matter which way the market is moving, God is always better than gold. Therefore, by God's help we can be and we should be content with the simple necessities of life.

Second, we can be content with simplicity because the deepest, most satisfying delights God gives us through creation are free gifts from nature and from loving relationships with people. After your basic needs are met, accumulated money begins to diminish your capacity for these pleasures rather than increase them. Buying things contributes absolutely nothing to the heart's capacity for joy.

There is a deep difference between the temporary thrill of a new toy and a homecoming hug from a devoted friend. Who do you think has the deepest, most satisfying joy in life, the man who pays $140 for a fortieth-floor suite downtown and spends his evening in the half-lit, smoke-filled lounge impressing strange women with ten-dollar cocktails, or the man who chooses the Motel 6 by a vacant lot of sunflowers and spends his evening watching the sunset and writing a love letter to his wife?

Third, we should be content with the simple necessities of life because we could invest the extra we make for what really counts. Three billion people today are outside Jesus Christ. Two-thirds of them have no viable Christian witness in their culture. If they are to hear—and Christ commands that they hear—then cross-cultural missionaries will have to be sent and paid for. All the wealth needed to send this new army of good news ambassadors is already in the church.

If we, like Paul, are content with the simple necessities of life, hundreds of millions of dollars in the church would be released to take the gospel to the frontiers. The revolution of joy and freedom it would cause at home would be the best local witness imaginable. The biblical call is that you can and ought to be content with life's simple necessities.

(3) The third reason not to pursue wealth is that the pursuit will end in the destruction of your life. This is the point of verses 9 and 10:

Those who desire to be rich fall into temptation, into a snare, into many senseless and hurtful desires that plunge men into ruin and destruction. For the love of money is the root of all evils. It is through this craving that some have wandered away from the faith and pierced their hearts with many pangs.

No Christian Hedonist wants to plunge into ruin and destruction and be pierced with many pangs. Therefore, no Christian Hedonist desires to be rich.

Test yourself. Have you learned your attitude toward money from the Bible, or have you absorbed it from contemporary American merchandising? When you ride an airplane and read the airline magazine, almost every page teaches and pushes a view of wealth exactly opposite from the view in 1 Timothy 6:9 that those desiring to be rich will fall into ruin and destruction. Paul makes vivid the peril of the same desire which the airline magazines exploit and promote.

I recall a full-page ad for a popular office chair which showed a man in a plush office. The ad's headline read, "His suits are custom tailored. His watch is solid gold. His office chair is_____."
Below the man's picture was this quote:

I've worked hard and had my share of luck: my business is a success. I wanted my office to reflect this and I think it does. For my chair I chose_____. It fits the image I wanted...If you can't say this about your office chair, isn't it about time you sat in a_____? After all, haven't you been without one long enough?

The philosophy of wealth in those lines goes like this: If you've earned them, you would be foolish to deny yourself the images of wealth. If 1 Timothy 6:9 is true, and the desire to be rich brings us into Satan's trap and the destruction of hell, then this advertisement, which exploits and promotes that desire, is just as destructive as anything you might read in the sex ads of a big city daily.

Are you awake and free from the false messages of American

merchandising? Or has the omnipresent economic lie deceived you so that the only sin you can imagine in relation to money is stealing? I believe in free speech and free enterprise because I have no faith whatsoever in the moral capacity of sinful civil government to improve upon the institutions created by sinful individuals. But for God's sake let us use our freedom as Christians to say *no* to the desire for riches and *yes* to the truth: There is great gain in godliness when we are content with the simple necessities of life.

WHAT SHOULD THE RICH DO?

So far we have been pondering the words addressed in 1 Timothy 6:6–10 to people who are not rich but who may be tempted to want to be rich. In 1 Timothy 6:17–19 Paul addresses a group in the church who are already rich. What should a rich person do with his money if he becomes a Christian? And what should a Christian do if God prospers his business so that great wealth is at his disposal? Paul answers like this:

> (17) As for the rich in this world, charge them not to be haughty, nor to set their hopes on uncertain riches but on God who richly furnishes us with everything to enjoy. (18) They are to do good, to be rich in good deeds, liberal and generous, (19) thus laying up for themselves a good foundation for the future, so that they may take hold of the life which is life indeed.

The words of verse 19 simply paraphrase Jesus' teaching. Jesus said:

> Do not lay up for yourselves treasures on earth, where moth and rust consume and where thieves break in and steal, but lay up for yourselves treasures in heaven, where neither moth nor rust consumes and where thieves do

not break in and steal. For where your treasure is, there will your heart be also. (Matthew 6:19–21)

Jesus is not against investment. He is against bad investment—namely, setting your heart on the comforts and securities that money can afford in this world. Money is to be invested for eternal yields in heaven—"Lay up for yourselves treasures in heaven!" How?

Luke 12:32–34 gives one answer:

Fear not, little flock, for it is your Father's good pleasure to give you the kingdom. Sell your possessions, and give alms; provide yourselves with purses that do not grow old, with a treasure in the heavens that does not fail, where no thief approaches and no moth destroys. For where your treasure is, there will your heart be also.

So the answer to how to lay up treasures in heaven is to spend your earthly treasures for merciful purposes in Christ's name here on earth. Give alms—that is, provide yourself with purses in heaven. Notice carefully that Jesus does not merely say that treasure in heaven will be the unexpected results of generosity on earth. No, he says we should pursue treasure in heaven. Lay it up! Provide yourselves with unfailing purses and treasures! This is pure Christian Hedonism.

Another instance of it in the teaching of Jesus is Luke 14:13–14, where he is more specific about how to use our resources to lay up treasures in heaven.

Whenever you give feast, invite the poor, the crippled, the lame and the blind, and you will be blessed, because they cannot pay you back, for it will be paid back to you in the resurrection of the just.

This is virtually the same as saying, "Give alms; provide yourselves purses in heaven." Don't seek the reward of an earthly tit for tat. Be generous. Don't pad your life with luxuries and comforts. Look to the resurrection and the great reward in God "whose presence is fulness of joy and at whose right hand are pleasures for evermore" (Psalm 16:11).

Beware of commentators who divert attention from the plain meaning of these texts. What would you think, for example, of the following typical comment on Luke 14:13–14: "The promise of reward for this kind of life is there as a fact. You do not live this way for the sake of reward. If you do you are not living in this way but in the old selfish way."[1]

Is this true—that we are selfish and not loving if we are motivated by the promised reward? If so, why did Jesus entice us by mentioning the reward, even giving it as the basis ("for") of our action? And what would this commentator say concerning Luke 12:33, where we are not told that reward will result from our giving alms, but we are told to actively seek to get the reward— "Provide yourselves with purposes!"?

And what would he say concerning the parable of the unrighteous steward (Luke 16:1–13), where Jesus concludes, "Make friends for yourselves by means of unrighteous mammon, so that when it fails they may receive you into the eternal habitations" (16:9)? The aim of this parable is to instruct the disciples in the right and loving use of worldly possessions. Jesus does not say the result of such use is to receive eternal habitations. He says, Make it your aim to secure an eternal habitation by the use of your possessions.

So it is simply wrong to say that Jesus does not want us to pursue the reward he promises. He commands that we pursue it (Luke 12:33; 16:9). More than forty times in the Gospel of Luke there are promises of reward and threats of punishment connected with the commands of Jesus.[2]

Of course, we must not seek the reward of earthly praise or

material gain. This is clear not only from Luke 14:14, but also from Luke 6:35, "Love your enemies, and do good, expecting nothing in return; and *your reward will be great, and you will be sons of the Most High.*" In other words, don't care about earthly reward; look to the heavenly reward, namely, the infinite joys of being a son of God!

Or, as Jesus put it in Matthew 6:3–4, don't care about human praise for your merciful acts. If that is your goal, that's all you will get, and that will be a pitiful reward compared to the reward of God. "When you give alms, do not let your left hand know what your right hand is doing, so that your alms may be in secret; and *your Father who sees in secret will reward you.*"

The reason our generosity toward others is not a sham-love when we are motivated by the longing for God's promise is that we are aiming to take those others with us into that reward. We know our joy in heaven will be greater if the people we treat with mercy are won over to the surpassing worth of Christ, and join us in praising him.

But how will we ever point them to Christ's infinite worth if we are not driven, in all we do, by the longing to have more of him? It would only be unloving if we pursued our joy at the expense of others. But if our very pursuit includes the pursuit of their joy, how is that selfish? How am I the less loving if my longing for God moves me to give away my earthly possessions so that my joy in him can be forever doubled in your partnership of praise?

Paul's teaching to the rich in 1 Timothy 6:19 continues and applies these teachings of Jesus from the Gospels. He says rich people should use their money in a way that "lays up for themselves a good foundation for the future and takes hold on life which is life indeed." In other words, there is a way to use your money that forfeits eternal life.[3]

We know Paul has eternal life in view because seven verses earlier he uses the same kind of expression in reference to eternal life: "Fight the good fight of faith; take hold of the eternal life to which you were called when you made the good confession in the presence of many witnesses" (1 Timothy 6:12).

The reason the use of your money provides a good foundation for eternal life is not that generosity earns eternal life, but that it shows where your heart is. Generosity confirms that our hope is in God and not in ourselves or our money. We don't earn eternal life. It is a gift of grace (2 Timothy 1:9). We receive it by resting in God's promise. Then how we use our money confirms or denies the reality of that rest.

Paul gives three directions to the rich about how to use their money to confirm their eternal future.

First, don't let your money produce pride. "As for the rich in this world, charge them not to be haughty" (1 Timothy 6:17). How deceptive our hearts are when it comes to money! Every one of us has felt the smug sense of superiority that creeps in after a clever investment or new purchase or a big deposit. Money's chief attraction is the power it gives and the pride it feeds. Paul says, don't let this happen.

Second, he adds in verse 17, "Don't set your hope on uncertain riches, but on God who richly furnishes you all things to enjoy." This is not easy for the rich to do. That's why Jesus said it is hard for a rich man to enter the kingdom of God (Mark 10:23). It is hard to look at all the earthly hope that riches offer and then turn away from that to God, and rest all your hope on him. It is hard not to love the gift instead of the Giver. But this is the only hope for the rich. If they can't do it, they are lost.

They must remember the warning Moses gave the people of Israel as they entered the promised land:

Beware lest you say in your heart, "My power and the might of my hand have gotten me this wealth." You shall remember the LORD your God, for it is he who gives you power to get wealth; that he may confirm his covenant which he swore to your fathers, as at this day. (Deuteronomy 8:17–18)

The great danger of riches is that our affections will be carried away from God to his gifts. Before moving on to Paul's third exhortation for the rich, we must consider a common abuse of verse 17. The verse says that "God richly furnishes us with everything to enjoy." This means, first, that God is usually generous in the provision he makes to meet our needs. He furnishes things "richly." Second, it means we need not feel guilty for enjoying the things he gives us. They are given "for enjoyment." Fasting, celibacy, and other forms of self-denial are right and good in the service of God, but they must not be elevated as the spiritual norm. The provisions of nature are given for our good and, by our Godward joy, can become occasions of thanksgiving and worship (1 Timothy 4:2–5).

But a wealth-and-prosperity doctrine is afoot today, shaped by the half-truth that says, "We glorify God with our money by enjoying thankfully all the things he enables us to buy. Why should a son of the King live like a pauper?" And so on. The true half of this is that we should give thanks for every good thing God enables us to have. That does glorify him. The false half is the subtle implication that God can be glorified in this way by all kinds of luxurious purchases.

If this were true, Jesus would not have said, "Sell your possessions and give alms" (Luke 12:33). He would not have said, "Do not seek what you are to eat and what you are to drink" (Luke 12:29). John the Baptist would not have said, "He who has two coats, let him share with who has none" (Luke 3:11). The Son of Man would not have walked around with no place to lay his head (Luke 9:58). And Zacchaeus would not have given half his goods to the poor (Luke 19:8).

God is not glorified when we keep for ourselves (no matter how thankfully) what we ought to be using to alleviate the misery of unevangelized, uneducated, unmedicated, and unfed millions. The evidence that many professing Christians have been deceived by this doctrine is how little they give and how much they own. God *has* prospered them. And by an almost irresistible law of consumer culture (baptized by a doctrine of health, wealth, and prosperity) they have bought bigger (and more) houses, newer (and more) cars, fancier (and more) clothes, better (and more) meat, and all manner of trinkets and gadgets and containers and devices and equipment to make life more fun.

They will object: Does not the Old Testament promise that God will prosper his people? Indeed! God increases our yield so that by giving we can prove our yield is not our god. God does not prosper a man's business so that he can move from a Ford to a Cadillac. God prospers a business so that 17,000 unreached peoples can be reached with the gospel. He prospers a business so that twelve percent of the world's population can move a step back from the precipice of starvation.

I am a pastor, not an economist. Therefore I see my role today the way James Stewart saw it in Scotland thirty years ago.

> It is the function of economists, not the pulpit, to work out plans of reconstruction. But it is emphatically the function of the pulpit to stab men broad awake to the terrible pity of Jesus, to expose their hearts to the constraint of that divine compassion which halos the oppressed and the suffering, and flames in judgment against every social wrong.... There is no room for a preaching devoid of ethical directness and social passion, in a day when heaven's trumpets sound and the Son of God goes forth to war.[4]

The mention of "war" is not merely rhetorical. What is specifically called for today is a "wartime lifestyle." I have used the phrase "simple necessities of life" earlier in this chapter because Paul said in 1 Timothy 6:8, "If we have food and clothing, with these we shall be content." But this idea of simplicity can be very misleading. I mean it to refer to a style of life that is unencumbered with nonessentials—and the criterion for "essential" should not be primitive "simplicity," but wartime effectiveness. Ralph Winter illustrates this idea of a wartime lifestyle:

> The *Queen Mary*, lying in repose in the harbor at Long Beach, California, is a fascinating museum of the past. Used both as a luxury liner in peacetime and a troop transport during the Second World War, its present status as a museum the length of three football fields affords a stunning contrast between the lifestyles appropriate in peace and war. On one side of a partition you see the dining room reconstructed to depict the peacetime table setting that was appropriate to the wealthy patrons of high culture for whom a dazzling array of knives and forks and spoons held no mysteries. On the other side of the partition the evidences of wartime austerities are in sharp contrast. One metal tray with indentations replaced fifteen plates and saucers. Bunks, not just double but eight tiers high, explain why the peacetime complement of 3000 gave way to 15,000 people on board in wartime. How repugnant to the peacetime masters this transformation must have been! To do it took a national emergency, of course. The survival of a nation depended upon it. The essence of the Great Commission today is that the survival of many millions of people depends on its fulfillment.[5]

There is a war going on. All talk of a Christian's right to live luxuriantly "as a child of the King" in this atmosphere sounds hollow—especially since the King himself is stripped for battle. It is more helpful to think of a "wartime" lifestyle than a merely "simple" lifestyle. Simplicity can be very inward directed, and may benefit no one else. A wartime lifestyle implies that there is a great and worthy cause for which to spend and be spent (2 Corinthians 12:15). Winter continues:

America today is a save-yourself society if there ever was one. But does it really work? The underdeveloped societies suffer from one set of diseases: tuberculosis, malnutrition, pneumonia, parasites, typhoid, cholera, typhus, etc. Affluent America has virtually invented a whole new set of diseases: obesity, arteriosclerosis, heart disease, strokes, lung cancer, venereal disease, cirrhosis of the liver, drug addiction, alcoholism, divorce, battered children, suicide, murder. Take your choice. Laborsaving machines have turned out to be body-killing devices. Our affluence has allowed both mobility and isolation of the nuclear family, and as a result our divorce courts, our prisons and our mental institutions are flooded. In saving ourselves we have nearly lost ourselves.

How hard have we tried to save others? Consider the fact that the U.S. evangelical slogan, "Pray, give, or go" allows people merely to pray, if that is their choice! By contrast the Friends Missionary Prayer Band of South India numbers 8,000 people in their prayer bands and supports 80 full-time missionaries in North India. If my denomination (with its unbelievably greater wealth per person) were to do that well, we would not be sending 500 missionaries, but 26,000. In spite of their true poverty, those poor people in South India are sending 50 times as many cross-cultural missionaries as we are.[6]

The point here is to show that those who encourage Christians to pursue a luxuriant peacetime lifestyle are missing the point of all Jesus taught about money. He called us to lose our lives in order that we might gain them again (and the context is indeed money—"What does it profit a man, to gain the whole world and forfeit his life?" (Mark 8:36). And the way he means for us to lose our lives is in fulfilling the mission of love he gave us.

Which leads us to the final admonition Paul makes to the rich: "They are to do good, to be rich in good deeds, liberal and generous" (1 Timothy 6:18). Once they are liberated from the magnet of pride and once their hope is set on God, not money, only one thing can happen: Their money will flow freely to multiply the manifold ministries of Christ.

So what does a pastor say to his people concerning the purchase and ownership of two homes in a world where 2,000 people starve to death every day and mission agencies cannot penetrate more unreached peoples for lack of funds? First, he may quote Amos 3:15—"I will smite the winter house and the summer house; and the houses of ivory shall perish; and the great houses shall come to an end." Then he may read Luke 3:11, "He who has two coats, let him share with him who has none."

Then he might tell about the family in St. Petersburg, Florida, who caught a vision for the housing needs of the poor. They sold their second home in Ohio and used the funds to build houses for several families in Immokalee, Florida.

Then he will ask, is it wrong to own a second home that sits empty part of the year? And he will answer, Maybe and maybe not. He will not make it easy by creating a law. Laws can be obeyed under constraint with no change of heart; prophets want new hearts for God, not just new real estate arrangements. He will empathize with their uncertainty and share his own struggle to discover the way of love. He will not presume to have a simple answer to every lifestyle question.

But he will help them decide. He will say, "Does your house signify or encourage a level of luxury enjoyed in heedless unconcern of the needs of others? Or is it a simple, oft-used retreat for needed rest and prayer and meditation that sends people back to the city with a passion to deny themselves for the evangelization of the unreached and the pursuit of justice?"

He will leave the arrow lodged in their conscience and challenge them to seek a lifestyle in sync with the teaching and life of the Lord Jesus.

WHY HAS GOD GIVEN US SO MUCH?

In Ephesians 4:28, Paul says, "Let the thief no longer steal, but rather let him labor, doing honest work with his hands, so that he may be able to give to those in need." In other words, there are three levels of how to live with things: (1) you can steal to get; (2) or you can work to get; (3) or you can work to get in order to give.

Too many professing Christians live on level two. Almost all the forces of our culture urge them to live on level two. But the Bible pushes us relentlessly to level three. "God is able to provide you with every blessing in abundance, so that you may always have enough of everything and may provide in abundance for every good work" (2 Corinthians 9:8). Why does God bless us with abundance? So we can have enough to live on and then use the rest for all manner of good works that alleviate spiritual and physical misery. Enough for us; abundance for others.

The issue is not how much a person makes. Big industry and big salaries are a fact of our times, and they are not necessarily evil. The evil is in being deceived into thinking a $100,000 salary must be accompanied by a $100,000 lifestyle. God has made us to be conduits of his grace. The danger is in thinking the conduit should be lined with gold. It shouldn't. Copper will do.

Our final summary emphasis should be this: In 1 Timothy 6, Paul's purpose is to help us lay hold on eternal life and not lose it. Paul never dabbles in unessentials. He lives on the brink of eternity. That's why he sees things so clearly. He stands there like God's gatekeeper and treats us like reasonable Christian Hedonists: You want life which is life indeed, don't you (verse 19)? You don't want ruin, destruction and pangs of heart, do you (verses 9–10)? You do want all the gain that godliness can bring, don't you (verse 6)? Then use the currency of Christian Hedonism wisely: do not desire to be rich, be content with the wartime necessities of life, set your hope fully on God, guard yourself from pride and let your joy in God overflow in a wealth of liberality to a lost and needy world.

1. T. W. Manson, *The Sayings of Jesus* (London: SCM Press, 1949), 280.

2. John Piper, *Love Your Enemies* (Cambridge: Cambridge University Press, 1979). On pages 163–65 I list and discuss these some forty instances.

3. This does not contradict the biblical doctrine of the eternal security of God's chosen people who are truly born again, a doctrine firmly established by Romans 8:30. But it does imply there is a change of heart if we have been born of God; and this includes evidences in the way we use our money. Jesus warned repeatedly of the false confidence that bears no fruit and will forfeit life in the end (Matthew 7:15–27, 13:47–50, 22:11–14).

4. James Stewart, *Heralds of God* (Grand Rapids, Mich.: Baker Book House, 1972), 97.

5. Ralph Winter, "Reconsecration to a Wartime, not a Peacetime, Lifestyle," in *Perspectives on the World Christian Movement*, ed. R. Winter and S. Hawthorne, (Pasadena, Calif.: William Carey Library, 1981), 814.

6. Winter, "Reconsecration," 815.

STRUGGLING

WITH

DEPRESSION

CHARLES M. SELL

Charles M. Sell
Professor, Trinity Seminary
Author and conference speaker

"As children of God we don't have to be depressed or defeated in life."[1] Is this true? Did the person who wrote those words have his head in the sand, the clouds, or the Bible? Does having a heavenly Father guarantee a heavenly disposition? When we travel the high road with God, will we never plod the low one?

The issue is crucial. One counselor friend of mine says half of his patients come to him because they are depressed. It is, in fact, the most common kind of abnormal behavior. Each of us has a one-in-ten chance of becoming severely depressed. And all of us have our regular skirmishes with its milder form.

Depression is a complicated matter. Experts are not agreed on what causes it. And getting over it is not simply a matter of "picking yourself up" or "snapping out of it." We simply do not have all the answers, and we should be very careful about offering "easy formulas" or "pat solutions" for such a complex reality.

Becoming a Christian is not a vaccination against depression. Christianity does not equal happiness. The church is not Gladsville. True, Christians are urged to rejoice. Yet Christian joy can sometimes be mixed with cheerless despondency. The apostle Peter knew Christians could experience joy and grief at the same time. "In this you greatly rejoice, even though now for a little while, if necessary, you have been distressed by various trials" (1 Peter 1:6, NASB).

Many Christians don't seem to think that way. As a fairly new Christian, I remember being surprised when my theology professor said: "Sometimes when you feel down, you don't need to pray more, you need a good night's sleep." His statement popped a guilt-filled balloon inside me. Somehow I had gotten the idea that I ought always to be "up."

Jesus, our example, was understandably "exceedingly sorrowful, even to the point of death," prior to His crucifixion. And down through the centuries many famous godly people have had noble bouts with mournful depression.

"My soul is downcast," said the weeping prophet, Jeremiah (Lamentations 3:20, NIV).

David complained: "My eyes grow weak with sorrow, my soul and my body with grief" (Psalm 31:9, NIV).

Martin Luther graphically described one of his frequent rock-bottom moods: "For more than a week I was close to the gates of death and hell. I trembled in all my members. Christ was wholly lost. I was shaken by desperation and blasphemy of God."[2]

Depression's victims include famous preacher Charles Spurgeon, Christian author C. S. Lewis, and poet Amy Carmichael.

The plight of Job, among the most notable sufferers, is the theme of the oldest book of the Bible. Job had plenty to sink his heart. In rapid succession he lost family, wealth, and health. After his wife advised, "Curse God and die," Job slipped quickly into a deep pit of despair.

JOB'S DEPRESSION TEST

Job's descriptions of despair are so accurate that you can use them to test your own emotional state. You can check yourself by marking the appropriate items.

Extreme sadness. "Why is light given to him who suffers, and life to the bitter of soul...?" (Job 3:20, NASB). Which is true of you? (a) I don't feel sad. (b) I am somewhat sad. (c) I am sad all the time and can't get over it. (d) I am so sad I am not sure I can stand it.

Sleep disturbance. "When I lie down I say, 'When shall I arise?' But the night continues, and I am continually tossing until dawn" (Job 7:4, NASB). Questions: (a) I do not find myself becoming more tired than usual. (b) I get tired more easily than I used to. (c) I get tired doing almost anything. (d) I am too tired to do anything.

Pessimism about life. "Man, who is born of woman, is short-lived and full of turmoil" (Job 14:1, NASB). (a) I am not particularly discouraged about the future. (b) I feel discouraged about the future. (c) I feel I have nothing to look forward to. (d) I feel the future is hopeless and that things cannot improve.

Life seems worthless. "I do not take notice of myself; I despise my life" (Job 9:21, NASB). (a) I get as much satisfaction out of things as I used to. (b) I don't enjoy things the way I used to. (c) I don't get real satisfaction out of anything anymore. (d) I am dissatisfied or bored with everything.

Helplessness. "I am not at ease, nor am I quiet, and I am not at rest, but turmoil comes" (Job 3:26, NASB). (a) I don't cry any more than usual. (b) I cry more now than I used to. (c) I cry all the time now. (d) I used to be able to cry, but now I can't cry even though I want to.

Physical signs of sadness. "My eye has also grown dim because of grief, and all my members are as a shadow" (Job 17:7, NASB). (a) My appetite is no worse than normal. (b) My appetite is not as good as it used to be. (c) My appetite is much worse now. (d) I have no appetite at all.

(a) I have not noticed any recent change in my interest in sex. (b) I am less interested in sex than I used to be. (c) I am much less interested in sex now. (d) I have lost interest in sex completely.

Desire for death. "Who long for death, but there is none, and dig for it more than for hidden treasures..." (Job 3:21, NASB). (a) I don't have thoughts of killing myself. (b) I have thoughts of killing myself, but I would not carry them out. (c) I would like to kill myself. (d) I would kill myself if I had the chance.[3]

Depression may also be marked by feelings of failure, lack of satisfaction, irritation, and loss of interest in people. This brief self check, however, is not intended to be absolutely accurate. It might signal your need to see a trained counselor and should not be used to replace going to one.

If you marked a lot of items with "a's" and a few "b's" depression is certainly not on your doorstep. If, however, you have a number of "c's" and a "d" or two, you have entered some sort of dark tunnel. A recent happening might explain it: a death of a loved one, the loss of a job or a friend. But if your glum mood begs for explanation, it is important for you to talk to a counselor. If you have any serious thought about taking your life, it is urgent that you talk with someone. And in the event that someone has confided to you thoughts about suicide, consider it an emergency—get them help now.

From time to time we have all had a lack of energy, a negative self-image, a sense of hopelessness, and other signs of depression. We can usually point to a clear-cut cause: recovery from an illness, exhaustion from hard work, a loss. These symptoms are part of grieving.

It may be normal to be in an emotional cellar even when some sobering event didn't shove you there. Depression can accompany a physical illness. A simple lack of exercise may be the culprit. And for many women, regular monthly blue periods are due to the menstrual cycle.

We can, however, distinguish between these so-called "normal," temporary bouts and depressive illness. By no means is the difference completely clear. Apparently there are some common elements in each. The "lows" are similar in three ways:

1. The descriptions of the negative feelings are much the

same: sadness, loneliness, and feelings of unworthiness.

2. The behavior of one matches the other: withdrawal from activity, weakness, and diminished sexual interest.

3. The physical reactions are similar: insomnia, fatigue, and loss of appetite.

Yet it is possible to tell one from the other. Normal depression does not incapacitate. That is, a person doesn't get to the place where he or she cannot work and fulfill expected responsibilities. This doesn't mean that the "normally" depressed might not be able to work for a time. We don't expect a grieving person to take up full responsibilities right away. But whenever an individual is not pulling his weight at a time when he should reasonably be expected to do so, something beyond the "normal" is happening.

Times of normal depression are also brief. Severe grieving usually lasts for a few months, though some internal sadness can continue for years. If extreme distress continues much longer than these few months—and seems to be getting worse—the sufferer may have a depressive illness.

One other distinguishing mark: the normally down-hearted retain a grasp on reality. They can usually experience and admit to some joy and beauty along with their moments of depression. Depressive illnesses, on the other hand, may plunge someone into such horrible darkness that the bleakness distorts their whole view of life. Looking back, one victim described the agony: "It was a horror and hell. I was at the bottom of the deepest pit there ever was. I was worthless and unforgivable. I was as good as—no, worse than—dead."[4]

When I was a young man, I tried to counsel with a woman in that state. Her shoulders drooped, her hands hung helplessly at her sides or else nervously twisted at her handkerchief. Deep, dark crescents under her eyes accented her melancholy look. Not understanding the extent of her illness, I tried to reason with her. "God has not forsaken you," I pleaded. "You are not damned as you now suspect." The positive, beautiful statements of God's grace and love from Scripture seemed incapable of penetrating her darkness as she cowered in the chair in the corner of the room. There was no reasoning with her. I could not point to facts and wholesome, uplifting ideas. To her, reality was a distorted gloom that tormented her and twisted her perception of life. Electroshock therapy lasting over a period of weeks made her see clearly once again. She was able to take hope from God's Word and the encouragement of loved ones.

Depressive illnesses are severe and life threatening.[5] According to Christian physician John White, they may take one of several forms.

Secondary depression. Depression that arises in the course of illness, or from conditions such as alcoholism, homosexuality, diabetes, and Cushing's syndrome. Remember there is usually some depression accompanying any injury or illness. It is the most common emotional response for both children and adults, often coming a few days after the injury or the onset of illness. When healing or recovery is slow or delayed, depression may set in.

Primary depression. This mood disorder cannot be associated with any other form of mental or physical illness. However, because we don't fully understand all of the relationships between physical illness and depression, it is difficult to make a distinction between primary and secondary depression.

Bipolar depression. These are primary depressions which are characterized not only by plunges into despair, but also by ascents into euphoria and even wild excitement.

Unipolar depression. These depressions do not combine highs and lows, but, as their name suggests, are plunges into darkness relieved only by normal moods.[6]

It would seem that depression, a condition so highly visible, ought to have a cause that is just as obvious. But this just isn't so. Cast a net out over the entire history of thinking about depression and you'll bring in numerous ideas about what's behind it.

It's crucial to look at these in an effort to understand depression. But it isn't always necessary to know the cause to prescribe a treatment. Depressive symptoms may be treated and vanish before anyone can pinpoint a cause.

Many of the following "causes" go a long way toward explaining both normal and severe depression. Just examining them might give you a clue to what gives you the blahs now and then. You might also gain some insight into the reasons for the depressive state of someone you're concerned about.[7]

Anger. It is common to think of depression as a form of anger turned inward. First introduced by Sigmund Freud, this theory is no longer adequate to explain serious depressive illness. It may account, however, for the so-called "normal" depressed mood we sometimes have.

When we get upset with someone we love, respect, or are afraid of, we may not *allow* ourselves to be angry with them. Perhaps the one stirring our ire is our spouse: we're afraid turning loose our anger will turn him or her away. Or the agitator could be a boss or relative. Showing our wrath might threaten to bring his wrath down on us. Perhaps guilt, not fear, keeps our anger in. We don't accept the rightfulness of anger. Or we simply can't justify being angry with someone we ought to love (as in the case of a teenager upset by a parent).

When the anger is kept in, it is sometimes *turned* in. The flow of bad feelings gushes back into our lives, like water streaming from a broken pipe. In short, we blame ourselves and end up feeling down about self, about life, and about the future. We feel lonely, sad, blue, guilty, and sometimes even lost and empty. And we often can't figure out why.

The despondency may very well melt away when we work it out or talk it out. It will fade even more quickly when we admit to ourselves we are mad at someone and handle it. Unadmitted anger is uncontrolled anger. Facing up to it is one way to get rid of it.

Loss. Bereavement can cause brief depression but can also trigger a depressive illness. What seems like a normal response becomes prolonged until the person is in a hopeless, helpless condition. Why this happens to some people is not absolutely certain. John White claims a lot of evidence proves previous losses can make a person "depressive prone." A traumatic event sends them into a nosedive. A person who has lost a parent in childhood, for instance, may be more susceptible to depression in adulthood. Studies shows that some persons (especially women) who are depression prone came from homes where parents fought a great deal.[8]

Inconsistent parental love can also be a factor. It is possible that these people grew up with a fear of traumatic detachment from parents which makes them susceptible to an onslaught of serious depression. We know parental affection in life's early years seems to contribute a great deal to later mental and emotional stability. When growing up we need to feel close to people and sense we belong. Early childhood experiences that make us feel neglected or rejected may not always cause depression in adulthood. However, being deprived of normal affection from parents and others might make a person prone to depression. Experts call this a "predisposing cause."

Old age. Depression is one of the most common complaints of the aged. Since older people endure so many losses, their depression is most likely a normal grief response, not an illness. Since aging itself does not cause depression, older persons with emotional disturbances should be treated like other age groups. Too often counseling is withheld from the elderly because they are thought to be incurable. Physicians may be inclined to treat them with drugs, believing the only goal is to give them an illusion of normalcy until they die. These drugs, often with harmful side effects, should not substitute for some attempt to help the older person cope with his moods and circumstances.

Loss of self-esteem. An exaggerated negative, punitive view of oneself is a symptom of depression. "Wretched, useless, helpless," are among the words the mirthless fling at themselves. Is this lack of self-esteem a cause of depression? Some experts think so. The feeling of helplessness and the loss of self-worth come first; the sadness and other gloom symptoms follow. The damaged self-respect usually comes when a person is unable to reach cherished ideals or goals. Naturally, this can be related to a loss. The lost job may mean one will never achieve his vocational goals. Or a lost loved one may trigger the sense of failure—a person may blame himself for the death. Or if he doesn't hold up well afterward, he may be severely disappointed with himself.

Because this guilt and lack of self-esteem are associated with depression, some people blame religion for contributing to the problem. From religion one may get unrealistic ideals, a low view of self, a strong concept of the necessity of punishment, and little assurance of forgiveness. Together they could cause depression. One counselor refers to this as "worm theology."[9] He points to lyrics of hymns to make his case: "such a worm as I," "wretch like me," "coming weak and vile," "poor, wretched, blind," "guilty, vile and helpless we."

No doubt this accusation contains some truth. Some Christians may not have enough exposure to the grace and love of God. Sin and failure lead them to collapse in depressive self-hatred. Misguided Christians may begin to equate sinfulness with worthlessness. They need to be reminded that all people are created in God's image. Scripture affirms that men and women are sinful, but it also affirms that we are not junk. Each individual is incalculably important to the Creator.

Sometimes Christians fall prey to false guilt. The individual continues to condemn himself for some wrong even when God has forgiven. It may very well be that nothing was done to require forgiveness in the first place.

The critical spirit of other Christians sometimes makes it difficult. Paul Tournier suggests that this pressure to "please others" is a basic factor in the creation of false guilt. True guilt comes from reproachment by God in our inner heart for sins we have committed. False guilt comes from judgments made by others—judgments which may or may not reflect the thoughts of God. The Bible is an all-important guide to the Christian in distinguishing between true and false guilt.[10]

It also helps to realize that *guilt may come from sources other than God.* Society, self, and Satan can induce it. The apostle Paul claims false prophets send people on guilt trips. Those who make unreasonable demands are said to give "attention to deceitful spirits and doctrines of demons..." (1 Timothy 4:1, NASB). This fits the biblical notion that Satan is an accuser of the brethren (Revelation 12:10).

Ask several questions to distinguish false from real guilt:

1. Can I trace my feelings to some disobedience against the clear teachings of Scripture?

2. Do my feelings relate in many ways to my past experiences as a child?

3. Do my guilt feelings persist after I have made a confession of my sin?

4. Are my feelings related to some unrealistic standards or goals I have set for myself?

5. Do I fear giving up my feelings of guilt? (Sometimes if we fail to feel guilty, we fear we may fail to achieve our goals. Such feelings of guilt are not the highest motivation for growing in the Christian life.)[11]

Sometimes we must let go of unrealistic standards that are beating us down and exchange less achievement for more peace of mind.

The theory that depression is caused by a lack of self-esteem has the chicken-egg problem. Is lack of self-worth the *cause* or the *symptom* of depression? Experts who deal with the severely depressed know that dealing with the guilt itself can be futile. The dark, dank mood swallows up arguments, Scripture verses, and other assurances of God's favor. Something else is causing the depression. When the bad mood goes away the good self-view will follow.

Hopelessness. Believing in mind over matter, some psychologists say depression is a problem with the mind, not the mood. The depressed person thinks too negatively about self, the present, and the future. Hopelessness sets in whenever that mindset occurs.

Change the mind, they say, and it will change the emotional state. This approach, called "rational therapy," has a lot to commend it, and has proven effective for many people. The treatment, however, is not as simple as it sounds. Rational therapists use numerous methods to treat the depressed; it's not merely a matter of telling persons to shape up or of talking them into a good view of life.

Anxiety. Depression, pure and simple, is a problem of being human. Life in general generates anxiety. Living becomes threatening or meaningless.

Perhaps there is more depression today because personal reasons for existence do not spring easily from modern life. We are bombarded by a confusing array of viewpoints which are devoid of any awareness of God. Without God and without hope is a cheerless state to be in. Add to this the everyday stresses and the threat of nuclear holocaust. In this, Jesus offers hope: "Be of good cheer, I have overcome the world" (John 16:33).

Brain chemistry. Just recently, psychologists have been made aware of the role of neurochemical balance in explaining and treating depression. It is quite clear that chemical changes in the brain occur simultaneously with depressive illness. But it is not clear that this is depression's cause. The question "which influences which?" is still unanswered.[12]

Brain chemistry is complex, as is the brain itself. The number of brain cells in each human equals the number of stars in our galaxy, about one hundred million. Communication has to go on between those cells. Sometimes the signals between them don't get through very well. Different things can go wrong. One of these hindrances has to do with the sodium chloride content within the cell. Because this salt plays a part in messages getting from cell to cell, something breaks down whenever the sodium ions and the chloride ions get out of balance. Sometimes the chemical problem is in another part of the cell.

Whenever there is a slowdown of cellular communication, memory and concentration can be affected. The transmitter problem, however, causes more trouble than this. It affects other glands of the body, making the overall condition a whole body chemistry matter.

Enormous numbers of people have been helped by doses of lithium (an inert salt) because it brings the sodium chloride back into balance. Certain antidepressant medications are used to treat other chemistry problems.

Demon possession. It's not hard to see how the gloom and doom aspects of depression can be closely associated with evil spiritual powers. Persons often feel as though they are in the grip of something they can't shake. When you see how helpless and tormented a dejected person sometimes is, it is very easy to suspect some lurking supernatural power is at work in them.

Because the New Testament confirms the reality of demon possession and oppression, demons can't be ruled out as a cause of depression. Contemporary Christians tell us of encounters with such cases.

But we must be cautious—extremely cautious—about labeling someone as "demon-possessed." What might initially appear to be a convenient diagnosis could turn out to be complicating—and damaging. Other causes ought to be first considered. Suppose a depression is induced by chemical changes or emotional turmoil? Efforts to cast out a demon will fail. The despondent person may be driven into greater depths of hopelessness when a supposed "demon" will not leave despite the prayers and efforts of Christian friends.

Blaming depression on a demon may not lead to an easy solution. Christ's apostles failed to cast out a demon on one embarrassing occasion. Some of these beings are apparently quite stubborn and powerful. Jesus identified the one that resisted the disciples as the kind that comes out "only by prayer" (Mark 9:14–29).

Whether or not we know the cause of a loved one's depression, we can still pray for his health. When his condition becomes severe, no matter whether we suspect demon activity or not, we should seek the help of a competent Christian psychologist.

TREATING DEPRESSION

It should be apparent by now that just as there is no one cause of depression, there will be no single treatment. Persons with depressive illnesses will not respond to being told to "snap out of it." Getting them to a competent professional counselor will be the kindest thing we can do for them.

The following suggestions are applicable to our normal, mild depressions as well as the more serious ones. Please note, however, that they may do little good for someone who is in a very low state. I offer these simply as potentially helpful guidelines. I have no intention of guaranteeing they will automatically lead everyone through the tunnel of gloom.

Getting the picture. See depression for what it is. When depressed, we picture ourselves in a "pit" or "black hole." We talk about "being down" and "going down." Why not think of it as a *tunnel*? Depression may not be something to climb out of as much as something to "go through." Like a tunnel, as soon as you enter depression, you are already on the way out. You may just be at the beginning. That's the bad news. But the good news is that you'll get through it. You'll see the light again.

For this reason, experts tell us depression can be good for us. It is a normal response to certain circumstances of life.

We *should* mourn when we sin. Sadness is a positive response to committing a crime or hurting someone. Those who don't know sorrow cannot say, "I'm sorry."

When crisis or loss crash into our lives, depression may be beneficial. Slowed down, we process our thoughts and reexamine our perspectives and values. Depression gives the feelings the chance to respond, to regroup, and to do whatever emotions do to heal themselves. Depression is a healing process, or, perhaps, the pain that the healing process generates. It is ultimately put to good use and becomes a source of personal growth.[13]

Despite the torment of his dark periods, Luther said, "Without them no man can understand Scripture, faith, the fear or the love of God."[14]

This does not mean that we nurture our depression. But it does mean that in some respects we can't fight it. Beating at it, frantically waving one's arms at the black vapor within the soul as if to drive it out, will not work.

What then do we do with depression? We live with it, doing what we can to eventually make it lift.

Beware the easy quick fix. Despondency can make us desperate. We grasp for any promising cure. It is easy to believe that something that worked for someone else will work for us. If we pray a certain prayer, the heaviness will lift. If we do a certain thing, relief will come.

We hear about people who seemed to find simple solutions and sudden, almost miraculous relief. We want the same. Several days ago I read about a pastor whose depression cost him his job and hospitalized him. After release from the hospital he went alone to a mountain cabin to think and pray. Meditation and Scripture convinced him his problem was related to a spiritual battle with Satan.

"Oh, God," he sobbed, "is this what is happening to me?" He told God he had ignored His help in overcoming his depression. Then, it happened. "I noticed as I remained there that things felt different." He recollected. "Nothing ecstatic or noisy. Nothing high-powered or sensational. I just felt different. As I examined that feeling, I became aware of the strength in my limbs, of objects before my eyes. I saw, I felt, I heard. Was it possible? Was the cloud finally gone? Had my world come alive again? I began thanking and praising God, singing and laughing."

He returned home a new man. In a few days his family was telling everyone: "Dad is finally out of his black hole. Dad's depression is gone."[15]

Reading this, a depressed person might easily think the same thing could happen to him. A simple prayer. A realization. A confession. A few days in a mountain cabin. It worked for him—maybe it will work for me.

The man who wrote that account would not want anyone to think that. He tells of the months of counseling, the weeks of hospitalization that were a prelude to his mountain-cabin experience. Perhaps some new realization turned the corner for him. Nevertheless, all of the previous agonizing, counseling, and hospitalization may have been necessary before the healing finally came. The mountain-top experience was only the last dose in the treatment...not the only one.

Share the load. Studies confirm that people who have someone to confide in are better able to handle life's stresses. Depression thrives on your keeping it to yourself. Admitting to others your honest feelings keeps you honest with yourself. It helps you think better and somehow opens holes to let out some of the gloom.

Grasp the feeling/thought connection. All parts of us are connected: body, emotions, and thoughts. Each acts on the other. The physical self can make the emotional self feel down, as everyone who has had the common cold knows. Likewise the emotional self can affect the mental self, making the mind churn out all kinds of ridiculous things. When depressed, Luther thought terrible things about God. In grief, C. S. Lewis tells how he pictured God as some sort of monster.

When our feelings are drooping we should realize that they are probably telling the mind what to think. Statements like "I am no good" or "I can't do anything right" or "God could never forgive *my* sin" aren't really what the intellect is saying. They are what the emotions are telling it to think. Negative feelings give birth to negative thoughts. We can't take these thoughts seriously.

When depression becomes an illness, a person is unable to control these thoughts and mistakenly takes them at face value. He loses touch with reality. It does little good to appeal to a person's thoughts when they have succumbed to the control of their dreary, morose feelings. Treatment with antidepressants or other therapy may be needed to transform the emotions and change the thoughts.

But this doesn't mean that we should stop reasoning and talking sense with depressed persons. We can work at generating right thinking.

While feelings can control our thoughts, it can be the other way around. We need to utilize our spiritual and mental resources when we are down. Fill the mind with positive thoughts even though the emotions are saying, "That's baloney."

Words about hope, grace, love, and forgiveness may not immediately pop us into heavenly sunshine. But the input is significant in the long run. Good music can soothe the feelings while cheerful lyrics can stimulate the mind.

Get the body moving. Action can be like medicine. Emotions respond to circumstances even when they don't heed our thoughts. Emotions are rebellious at times. They won't take orders. They easily ignore commands such as "Stop being angry" or "Don't feel sad" or "Be happy."

Nevertheless, our *will* can handle emotions when the thoughts can't. When we feel blue, we can ask our will to do something about it. "Will," we can say, "take the body out where there is a chance the emotions will start feeling better."

Psychologist William James maintained that our emotions are

closely connected to our actions. We are afraid, he would say, because we are acting frightened. We've all experienced this at the swimming pool. As we lie in the sun, our emotions aren't up to a jump into the cold water. We may try without success to convince our emotions to rise to the occasion. But then "will" takes over. We jump into the water and start swimming. Suddenly we *feel* like swimming. William James would explain that you feel like swimming because you are doing it. That reverses the usual notion: that we swim because we feel like it.

To paraphrase James, we would help ourselves out of depression by doing nondepressive things—even if we don't feel like doing them.

Martin Luther also suggested some down-to-earth cures for depression. He advised people with mild bouts to ignore the heaviness. Luther counseled sufferers to shun solitude and seek the warm company of friends, discussing irrelevant matters. "A good way to exorcise the Devil," he maintained, "was to harness the horses and spread manure on the fields."[16]

Physical exercise seems to be a universal treatment for depression, no matter how severe that depression may be. Granted, the thought of jogging around the block may make someone more depressed. But it is important to begin doing something to get the heart and blood and muscles working. Even with a short walk, you will get started toward more walking. And that's progress.

Perhaps one of the reasons physical exercise works so well is that it gives a person some control over his life and circumstances. One of the marks of depression is a morbid fear about the helplessness of the situation. The future seems bleak; nothing can be done to change the present. This attitude needs to be changed. Doing something that makes you feel in control is a way of doing that.

A psychologist treats the depressed by helping them consider what project they would like to undertake. Sometimes they want to do something about the weight they've gained. Starting an exercise program and a diet can be a step toward regaining the sense of mastery that seems to be lost. This becomes the first step out of the pit.

Exercise three-way trust. What does confronting depression mean for the believer? Does it mean "facing it" or *"faithing it"*? If Scripture says the just shall live by faith, it implies that the depressed will get through by faith. Not that practical and even medical treatments are unnecessary. It's just that these should be undergirded and upheld by trust in a faithful God.

1. Trust means relying on God's power rather than on our strength. "Our competence comes from God" (2 Corinthians 3:4). There is relief for those who "take their hands off their own lives and fall into God's arms." No matter how you got into the tunnel, let God bring you out.

2. Trust means relying on God's mercy and grace. "For it is by grace you have been saved, through faith," Scripture reminds us, "and this not from yourselves, it is the gift of God—it is not by works..." (Ephesians 2:8–9, NIV). This is a radical thought. It means that I did nothing to make God love me. Therefore, I can do nothing to make Him love me more. And I can do nothing wrong to make Him love me less. Committed to a Savior who died for our sins, we can rely on God's grace.

3. Trust means hoping. Contemplating his own depressed heart, the psalmist asked himself, "Why are you downcast, O my soul? Why so disturbed within me?" Without waiting for an answer, he told himself: "Put your hope in God..." (Psalm 42:5, NIV).

Once my wife, Ginger, showed me a verse of Scripture that had helped carry her through a few years ago. We were delightfully astonished. Without her knowing it, I too had found that same statement of Scripture and was often turning it over in my mind during the same period of distress. It was Psalm 30:5: "Weeping may remain for a night, but rejoicing comes in the morning."

This thought may not stop our weeping. It may not sweep

away our despair. *But it can make us weep and despair in hope.* There is morning ahead.

The severely depressed man I mentioned earlier found this out. Joyless, dejected, he eventually sprawled on the carpet in his office. He was hopelessly unable to face even the simplest task. His helpless wife admitted him to a hospital psychiatric ward. At the time, he felt nothing positive, saw no bright spot. After doctors examined him, one of them said some gentle words—words he later said he would always be grateful for.

"Sir, you are deeply depressed—you need help—but you'll get better. It will take time...but you'll get better."[17]

Hope is not just the light at the end of the tunnel of gloom. It is the one sure light in the darkest part of it.

You'll get through.

1. Bob George, "There's No Need to Be Depressed," *Moody Monthly,* February, 1982: 7.

2. From Roland Bainton, *Here I Stand* (Nashville, Tenn.: Abingdon, 1950), 36.

3. Questions are adapted from "Becks Inventory for Measuring Depression" (University of Pennsylvania Press, 1967).

4. In John Altrocchi, *Abnormal Behavior* (New York: Harcourt Brace Jovanovich, 1980), 56.

5. John White, *The Masks of Melancholy* (Downers Grove, Ill.: InterVarsity Press, 1982), 63.

6. White, *Masks of Melancholy,* 63.

7. T. McKinney, "Overview of Recent Research in Depression: Integration of Ten Conceptual Models into a Comprehensive Clinical Frame," *Archives* 32 (1975): 285–305; and "Depressive Disorders: Toward a Unified Hypothesis," *Science* 182 (October 1974): 20–29. In White, *Masks of Melancholy,* 104–40.

8. *Journal of Abnormal Psychology,* vol. 88, no. 4 (1979): 398–406.

9. Dwight W. Cumbee, "Depression as an Ecclesiogenic Neurosis," *The Journal of Pastoral Care,* vol. XXXIV, no. 4 (December 1980): 259.

10. Paul Tournier, *Guilt and Grace* (New York: Harper & Row, 1962), 67.

11. Lloyd M. Perry and Charles M. Sell, *Speaking to Life's Problems* (Chicago: Moody Press, 1983), 146–47.

12. Richard E. Keady, "Depression, Psychophysiology and Concepts of God," *Encounter* 41 (Summer 1980), 265.

13. Keady, "Depression," 265.

14. Smiley Blanton, *Love or Perish* (New York: Simon and Schuster, 1956), 36.

15. Don Baker and Emery Nester, *Depression: Finding Hope and Meaning in Life's Darkest Shadow* (Portland, Oreg.: Multnomah Press, 1983), 101–3.

16. Bainton, *Here I Stand,* 364.

17. Baker and Nester, *Depression,* 20.

STRUGGLING

WITH

SELF-IMAGE

TONY CAMPOLO

Tony Campolo
Professor at Eastern College
Popular speaker and author

A friend of mine has an adorable four-year-old daughter. She is bright, and she is talkative. If tryouts were being held for a modern-day Shirley Temple, I think she would win, hands down.

One night there was a violent thunderstorm. The lightning flashed and the thunder rumbled—it was one of those terrifying storms that forces everyone to stop and tremble a bit. My friend ran upstairs to his daughter's bedroom to see if she was frightened and to assure her that everything would be all right. He got to her room and found her standing on the windowsill, spread-eagled against the glass. When he shouted, "What are you doing?" she turned away from the flashing lightning and happily reported, "I think that God is trying to take my picture."

Why don't most people feel that important—that good about themselves? Why don't most people like themselves as much as that little girl likes herself? Why are so many people down on themselves, and why do some even hate themselves?

I find that there is not too much correlation between people's circumstances and accomplishments and their self-concepts. I know people who definitely are socially successful, having achieved a significant number of worthwhile things in their lives, and who despise themselves. Contrariwise, I know others who by societal standards have not accomplished much at all, but who think of themselves as worthwhile and valuable.

Having a positive self-concept is of great importance not only for our own sense of well-being but for the well-being of all of those whom we meet in our everyday activities. I have found that people who like themselves are people who like everyone else they meet, and that those who are down on themselves are down on everyone else.

Check out this thesis in your own experience: Is it not true that the people you know who are always saying positive things about those with whom they live and work are the ones who basically feel good about themselves? And is it not also true in your experience that those who are nasty to others are themselves filled with self-contempt?

Part of what makes us feel bad about ourselves can be traced back to the ways we think we are viewed by the people around us, particularly those people who play the most important roles in our lives. Your husband or your wife, for instance, can make you feel wonderful about yourself, but he or she is also capable of cutting your sense of self-worth down to nothing. Parents and close friends can do this, too. I have often watched people destroy the self-esteem of a loved one right before my eyes.

A few months ago, I was a guest speaker for a citywide evangelistic service. Thousands of people were present, and there was a euphoric quality to the gathering. The excitement of the crowd and the presence of the Holy Spirit made the evening a memorable and blessed time.

When the service was over, a middle-aged couple pulled me aside to talk. Or perhaps I should say that the *wife* got me aside to talk—because she was the one who did all the talking. She gushed all over me and told me how wonderful I was, and she remarked that it must be very exciting for my wife to be married to me. All of that flattery made me a bit uneasy. But what really upset me was her not-too-subtle implication that the man to whom she was married, was, by comparison, rather boring. I felt that, while flattering me, she was simultaneously putting down her husband. By the end of her effusive praise, I wondered not only how her husband felt about me, but also how he felt about himself.

Of course, there are also many ways in which men put down their wives. One of the most evil side effects of soft porn magazines like *Playboy* is that the wives of those men who are "into" centerfolds are often made to feel that their husbands find them relatively unattractive. Middle-aged women are especially prone to a sense of self-contempt about their physical appearance because our culture defines beauty in very sexist and youth-oriented ways.

I do a bit of consulting work with my good friend Wayne Alderson's Value of the Person, a labor/management team that helps industries apply Christian principles to the activities of the workplace. Wayne has let me know that the complaint most often voiced by workers is over put-downs that come from bosses. He contends that most employers seem afraid to give affirmation and to make workers feel special and important. From his observations, it seems as though most employers try to convey to their workers that because they are easily replaceable, they had better be careful and do what they are told.

Wayne contends that because workers are often made to feel that they are valueless, they usually want union leaders who are tough and demanding with management. Without a personal sense of being valuable, workers can equate their worth only by how much money they can earn and how much security they can write into contracts.

According to Wayne, such feelings are the reason most relationships between workers and management go sour. Workers who have been regularly put down by their employers use union negotiations as opportunities to send a message to management that they are men and women and not simply things to be pushed around like machines. They are using the only means available to them to say that they are persons who are worth something.

At Value of the Person labor/management seminars, management and union members are brought together to express their feelings about themselves and each other. I will never forget attending one of these get-togethers at which a huge steelworker broke down and cried. The sight of this hulk of a man staring at the floor, his body trembling, brushing tears away from his cheeks is etched indelibly on my mind. I can still hear him saying, "You guys in management make me feel like s___!" While four-letter words are not as likely to be used by those of us proper types who go to offices each day, many of us can identify with that steelworker's feelings, because we feel exactly the same way in our own jobs.

Whatever others may do to us and to our self-images, many of us are filled with self-contempt because of what we do to ourselves. We do not have to experience put-downs from others to feel bad about ourselves; most of us can do a pretty good job of self-deprecation without any outside assistance.

Sometimes we even put ourselves down for religious reasons. There are times when our religion makes us too introspective for our own good. Spending more time than we should trying to discover all the sins in our lives can guarantee that we will end up depressed. If we concentrate too much on rooting out the evil that lies within us, we will find much more than we can handle.

I am not suggesting that we should ignore our sin, but I do believe that we should come to enjoy the grace of God. When Jesus died on the cross, He took *all* of our sin upon Himself— even those sins which we may have forgotten. According to the gospel, Jesus experienced on the cross all the condemnation necessary for what we have been and what we have done. Instead of condemning ourselves, therefore, we should bask in the good news that "there is therefore now no condemnation to them which are in Christ Jesus..." (Romans 8:1, KJV). If Christ has delivered us from condemnation, then we have no right to be down on ourselves. Having cast our sins upon Jesus, we ought to leave them behind and begin to press on to see ourselves in a positive light (Philippians 3:13–14, KJV).

Sigmund Freud once made the statement that the church is in the business of delivering people from guilt, but that if people do not *feel* guilt, then the church makes it its duty to *create* guilt. That way, the church can deliver people from what it has made them feel. Unfortunately, the church usually does a much better job of creating guilt than it does in providing deliverance from it.

I think that Freud was partly right. Too often we have allowed ourselves to be subject to a brand of Christianity that makes more of our sinfulness than it does of God's grace. We must know that "where sin abounded, grace did much more abound..." (Romans 5:20, KJV).

A lot of people criticize the popular television preacher Robert Schuller, claiming that he does not adequately point out that we are sinners. The truth is that Schuller *does* point out sin for his listeners, but he puts more of an emphasis on the grace of God. Schuller is able to help people feel good about themselves by convincing them that in Christ, they are not condemned for their sinfulness, but loved for their wonderful possibilities.

A prominent preacher in the Philadelphia area became involved with another man's wife. A divorce resulted, and the preacher lost his pulpit. As he picked up the pieces of his life and tried to put them back together again, I met with him occasionally to see how he was doing and try to be of some help. One day I asked him if he had found himself a new church home where he could worship and grow. He told me that he did not go to church anymore, but that he did listen regularly to Robert Schuller. I was surprised at his response, but he went on to say, "When a person has been through what I have been through, he doesn't need to be told that he's a sinner. He needs to hear that by the grace of God he has great possibilities, and that is what Schuller tells me."

I do not want to go on and on about Schuller here. But I do believe he has latched on to a powerful psychological and spiritual truth: Too much negative introspection in an effort to achieve some kind of spiritual perfection can do a terrible job on us! We need to remind ourselves, as Scripture reminds us, that God's grace has given us wonderful possibilities.

But as many as received him, to them gave he power to become the sons of God, even to them that believe on his name... (John 1:12, KJV)

Beloved, now are we the sons of God, and it doth not yet appear what we shall be: but we know that, when he shall appear, we shall be like him; for we shall see him as he is. (1 John 3:2, KJV)

Another way in which we often do a negative job on ourselves is by failing to take care of ourselves physically. There is a close connection between our physical well-being and our spiritual and psychological well-being. If we allow ourselves to get overtired or rundown, chances are we will end up depressed and maybe even hating ourselves.

I tend to be prone to this kind of self-induced physical abuse. Sometimes I overextend myself, work too hard, or try to accomplish too much, and end up physically exhausted. What is worse, in order to keep myself going, I sometimes drink several cups of coffee a day and eat candy bars to get quick bursts of energy. Naturally, all of this sets me up for depression. I am left not only feeling physically down, but also telling myself what a lousy person I am. My dilapidated condition not only makes me hard on myself, it makes me hard on everybody else around me. Self-contempt always leads to contempt for others.

If you find that you are really down on yourself, take some time off, rest up, check your diet, and make sure that the cause of how you feel is not self-inflicted physical abuse. Make sure that your body, which is "the temple of God," is treated with loving respect. You and everybody around you will suffer if you don't.

Self-contempt also can come from wasting time. Have you ever had a day off and wasted it on something as meaningless as watching hours of television or just sitting around doing nothing? Do you recall how you felt at the end of the day?—probably depressed and a bit down on yourself! If you repeated that kind of thing for several days in a row, you might really end up with a good dose of self-contempt. Wasting time may be one of the most devastating consequences of being on welfare. If you just sit around being lazy week after week because you have nothing of worth to do with your time, you will probably end up hating yourself—and others.

Activities which can alleviate a sense of wasting time are manifold. The easiest thing to do is to learn something. A day spent adding to your storehouse of knowledge is a day that will end up giving you a sense of accomplishment and well-being. To learn something new and important is to guarantee that you will feel good about yourself. For example, many retired people have been able to overcome the sense of worthlessness that sometimes accompanies inactivity by going back to college or taking classes at a community center.

In the Hebraic traction, learning the Torah was considered to be an end in itself, and those who were able to spend their time learning the things of God thought themselves to be very fortunate. There is much about that ancient Hebraic tradition which is applicable to our own lives. If you are down on yourself and you have the time, go back to school and learn about the things of God. Perhaps there is a Bible college or seminary nearby that has an adult education program. If not, try the community college in your area and take some religion or philosophy courses there. Learning about God is great therapy for those who have the need to improve the way they feel about themselves. So is learning about all that is in the world He has given us. As T. H. White wrote in *The Once and Future King,*

> The best thing for being sad...is to learn something. That is the only thing that never fails. You may grow old and trembling in your anatomies, you may lie awake at night listening to the disorder of your veins, you may miss your only love, you may see the world about you devastated by evil lunatics, or know your honour trampled in the sewers of baser minds. There is only one thing for it then—to learn. Learn why the world wags and what wags it.[1]

Doing good and serving others are other ways out of the doldrums of self-contempt. The missionary organization which I helped to establish, the Evangelical Association for the Promotion of Education, has an outreach program among urban children who are having problems with their schoolwork. In order to help these children, our organization enlists people to tutor them and to help them with their homework.

As we did our initial recruiting, we were able to find a half-dozen very well-educated women who were free and willing to help us in our efforts. Two of them were in psychotherapy because their negative feelings about themselves were so severe. But these two women were in for a surprising transformation. As they helped troubled inner-city children, they themselves found help. In serving the children, they began to sense their own worth. Doing something important for others made them feel that *they* were important. One of the women who had been in psychotherapy acknowledged that working with the kids had done more good for her than had her therapist. It was what she had done for others that was her psychological salvation. I am sure that Jesus had this in mind when He said,

> For whosoever will save his life shall lose it: and whosoever

will lose his life for my sake shall find it. For what is a man profited, if he shall gain the whole world, and lose his own soul? or what shall a man give in exchange for his soul? (Matthew 16:25–26, KJV)

I can never understand why people who are down on themselves do not grasp how easy it is to redefine their worth through meaningful service to others. There are always lonely people to be visited, visitation evangelism to be done, and children who need loving attention. I know that if those who are depressed would forget themselves (as Jesus suggests) and lose themselves in other people who need them, they would realize a great sense of self-worth.

There are a host of opportunities for short-term missionary work with periods of service that run from as short as two weeks to as long as two years. There are openings in various countries around the world as well as within the United States. My own missionary organization serves as a clearinghouse for persons who are looking for places where they can make long-lasting and important contributions for Christ and His kingdom. If you do not know where to turn for short-term missionary assignments, just write to me at:

The Evangelical Association for the Promotion of Education (EAPE)
Box 238
St. Davids, Pennsylvania 19087

People on my staff will be more than happy to help you to find a place where you can do for others the things that will insure your own sense of positive self-worth.

One final thing that can help if you are down on yourself is to try to recover the dreams of your childhood. Think back to when you had a vision for doing something wonderful with your life. All of us have unrealized dreams. Each of us can think of something glorious we "should have done" with our lives. Reconsider the options abandoned. Take another look at what might have been. Perhaps one of the reasons you are down on yourself is that you are angry with yourself for not stepping out and taking a good shot at fulfilling your own hopes for life. The dream that was once your own may have been given to you by God.

So often people tell me that they hate themselves because they have failed to become what they once hoped to be. Those who say such things reproach themselves most because they have never even tried. My advice to all such reluctant dreamers is "Go for it!" It is never too late. One of the advantages of long life expectancy most Americans enjoy today is that it is possible to attempt several vocations before our lives are ended. Having earned the money to put the kids through school, why not spend the rest of your life living out the impossible dream that you have secretly entertained for years?

I was preaching at a church one evening and really hitting on this theme. I told about Abraham who, "when his life was far spent," made the decision to live out the vision that God had given him. I pointed out that the entire eleventh chapter of Hebrews is nothing more than a listing of men and women who risked everything, including looking foolish, in order to respond to the dreams which God had placed in their hearts and minds. Faith, I declared, is nothing more and nothing less than believing that with God all things are possible—even careers of service when others are expecting you to retire.

When I was finished speaking, I felt that God had touched some hearts. This feeling was confirmed when a middle-aged couple came up to talk to me about their lives. That conversation led them to make some important decisions. And today that couple is part of a missionary team working in Paterson, New Jersey. They are helping some of the most disadvantaged children in America to find Christ and to have better lives. There is no doubt in my mind that this husband and wife feel terrific about themselves.

If your self-esteem is lagging, why don't you try something daring? If you do not take risks in living, you may risk not living at all. Once, when they asked Helen Keller if there was anything she could think of that was worse than being blind, she answered, "Yes! Being able to see and having no vision."

1. Terence H. White, *The Once and Future King* (New York: G. P. Putnam's Sons/Berkley Medallion Books, 1966), 183.

STRUGGLING

WITH

TRADITIONAL VALUES

CHARLES W. COLSON

Charles W. Colson
Founder and chairman of Prison Fellowship Ministries
1993 recipient of Templeton Prize for Progressive Religion
Author, speaker, columnist

THE FAMILY GAP

Parents As a Power Bloc

Political pundits have talked for several years about a gender gap—a difference in political opinions between men and women. But recently pollsters announced the discovery of a much larger difference.

They're calling it a family gap.

A *Reader's Digest* opinion poll shows that on cultural values, a deep split divides voters with children from voters without children—whether the latter are single or married.

Take, for example, the issue of abortion: only 48 percent of parents favor abortion, compared to 64 percent of married couples without children and a whopping 72 percent of singles.

On the issue of working mothers: A huge 74 percent of parents approve of mothers staying home with young children, compared to 53 percent of singles and 54 percent of married couples without children.

On homosexuality: Only 28 percent of parents believe homosexuals have a right to marry, compared to 46 percent of singles and 44 percent of married couples without children.

Asked to choose a political label, 64 percent of parents said conservative, compared to 45 percent of singles and 49 percent of married couples without children.

This striking gap holds across lines of age, gender, income, and region. The only factor affecting it is race. On several issues, black parents are even more conservative than white parents. On drugs, for example, 18 percent of white parents favor legalizing marijuana, but among black parents the number drops to 4 percent.

Political analysts consider a five-to-ten-point gap in the opinions of population groups to be significant. But the *Reader's Digest* poll found that on several issues the family gap tops twenty points—much higher than the gender gap ever was.

How can we explain the family gap?

It seems that the experience of parenthood itself deepens and matures young adults. The responsibility, the sacrifice, the commitment, and the new sense of the future all combine to shape parents' attitudes on key moral issues.

Psychologists used to speak as though all our development took place in the growing-up years. Toilet training and thumb sucking seemed to set a person's character for life. But today psychologists view all of life as a series of developmental steps to maturity—from youth, to marriage, to raising a family, and finally old age.

This doesn't mean everyone has to marry and have children in order to become mature, of course. Some of us have no choice in these matters. But generally speaking, those who follow the normal adult pattern are statistically more likely to develop mature character than those who choose a prolonged Yuppie adolescence.

Once again we see the wisdom of the biblical ethic, which

upholds marriage and the family. Not only because it's the best arrangement for raising children, but also because it's a way for adults to build strong character.

We've heard a lot over the years about the silent majority and the moral majority. But the real untapped political power in America today may be held by the parent majority.

POLITICALLY CORRECT TELEVISION

Numbing Our Minds with Numbers

Political correctness—PC. First it hit college campuses. Now it's hitting television. The networks are using prime-time programming to promote politically correct issues.

In PC television, we're treated to programs like "The Torkelsons," a show about single-parent families. What a contrast to the 1950s, when millions of Americans gathered around their black-and-white television sets to watch Ozzie and Harriet Nelson and their two sons.

Ozzie and Harriet became a symbol for the traditional family.

But now we're told that the traditional family is gone. Television must portray what are called "new social realities." The executive director for "The Torkelsons" told reporters that, after all, only one in ten American families is traditional anymore.

One in ten?

Statistics can be used to prove anything, it is said. And this is a prime example. Because that statistic is as cooked as any I've seen.

Let's analyze it. According to the Family Research Council, the 10 percent figure is based on any artificially narrow definition of the traditional family: one where Dad works, Mom's a housewife, and they have two—just two—children at home.

But this definition excludes all kinds of people who aspire to traditional family values.

It excludes young couples, whose family is still in the planning stage.

It excludes families where the mother works part time.

It excludes people like ex-President and Mrs. Bush, who are quite traditional but have more than two children.

It excludes grandmothers and grandfathers whose children are grown and married.

What about you? Does *your* family fall within the narrow definition of breadwinner, full-time homemaker, and precisely two children at home? If not, you and yours are lumped in the same category as homosexual couples, unmarried partners, and communes.

My own family suffers the same fate. I have three children instead of two, and they've married and moved out.

Since the sexual revolution of the sixties, the number of traditional families has declined. But it remains a lot higher than 10 percent.

So why was the statistic cooked up?

It seems almost deliberately contrived to make people *think* the traditional family is becoming extinct. There's no doubt that certain folks would *like* to see the family die out: gay rights activists, radical feminists, and sexual libertines. And if they can make it *look* that way, well, they've won half the battle.

People are less motivated to fight for a losing cause. If they *think* traditional families are only a fraction of the population, then government policy and public opinion will eventually become more accepting of alternative lifestyles. Even Christians may find it harder to sacrifice to do what's right if they think they stand alone.

So the next time you hear some expert cite that 10 percent statistic, don't be taken in. Remember it's based on an artificial definition of the family.

The truth is that a majority of Americans hold traditional values regarding family life. The good news is that this majority seems to be growing. *Fortune* magazine recently ran a computer analysis and discovered a burst of stories about the comeback of the traditional family. As the baby boomers mature, it seems they are rediscovering the wisdom of committed, stable family life. PC television may be doing its part to help do the family in. And "The Torkelsons" may be showing on the screen. But the folks in their living rooms watching it are beginning to look more like Ozzie and Harriet.

How Do You Define "Family Values"?

Something to Aspire To

Family values—it's the latest slogan to emerge from presidential politics. And the media is going haywire over it. At the 1992 Republican convention, reporters scurried about asking people what *they* thought family values were—and then gleefully concluded that no two people gave the same answer.

It seemed no one could define what the phrase means. Even Barbara Bush seemed a bit confused, saying in her speech, "However *you* define family, that's what we mean by family values."

With all due respect, Mrs. Bush was way off the mark. Family values are simply those values and beliefs that support the family.

Scripture teaches that God created the family to be one man, one woman, living in faithful love and raising their children. Families are the first community we live in, where we learn the most basic values. If we look at history, this has been the pattern for all stable societies.

Of course, in a fallen world we all fail in some ways to live up to the biblical norm. All around us we see struggling families, loveless families, and broken families. But the fact that some people don't live up to an ideal doesn't mean we should throw it out.

That would leave us with nothing to aspire to.

And yes, most people still aspire to the model set by the traditional family. Parents who adopt children resolve to treat them just *as if* they were their biological children. Single mothers look for men to act as father figures for their children.

The truth is that the traditional family at its best is the ideal *all* families aspire to.

But, of course, in today's culture it is no longer polite to say so. Society has drifted so far from any absolute standards that many people refuse to commit themselves to any single ideal for the family. School textbooks teach children that a family is any voluntary group of people living together. Holding to a single definition of the family is denounced as harsh, exclusive, and discriminatory.

In a way, holding on to biblical standards *is* discriminatory—not in the sense of discriminating against *people* but discriminating between *ideas*. The Bible teaches that it's good to be faithful to your spouse and wrong to be unfaithful. The Bible teaches that it's good to love and support your children and wrong to abuse or abandon them.

These are moral discriminations we *must* make in order to have healthy families. They are not optional. They are part of the moral order of the universe.

But they are exactly the kind of moral distinctions modern people resist making. They prefer a fuzzy sort of thinking that blurs all moral distinctions. One psychologist said, "Family values is the great Rorschach blot of American politics....People bring their own meanings to it."

This is total relativism—much like Barbara Bush's comment that a family is whatever you define it to be. And there is no more potent prescription for moral and family chaos.

CANDICE BERGEN'S FAMILY VALUES

Merely Personal Standards

I wager nearly half the country tuned in to the 1992 season's opening of "Murphy Brown." We all listened as Candice Bergen looked straight into the camera and told us that there is no normative definition of the family, that all that matters is "commitment, love, and caring."

But the fascinating thing is that Candice Bergen herself is actually very much in favor of family values.

That's right. Listen to what Bergen told *TV Guide* in an interview. "As far as my family values go," Bergen said, "my child and my family have always been my top priority....I don't see the point in having a child if you're not going to spend as much time as you can with that child."

These are strong words, but there's more. Bergen claimed that during the filming of the notorious episode when Murphy Brown had her baby, she herself had warned the producer about the implicit message the show might send.

Let me quote again from the *TV Guide* interview: "I said we do have to be careful," Bergen said, "that we don't send out the message...to young women especially, that we're encouraging them to be single mothers."

And she ended up saying, "I myself...believe the ideal is that you have a two-parent family. I'm the last person to think fathers are obsolete."

When I read that I was bowled over. Wow, I thought, so Candice Bergen really believes the two-parent family is the ideal? *Then why was she so opposed to Dan Quayle saying exactly the same thing?*

The answer is subtle, so listen carefully. We live in an age of individualism, where it's OK to be in favor of family values and marriage and all sorts of wonderful things—just so long as you make it clear that these are only your own private opinions. When Candice Bergen told us her family ideals, all she was doing was expressing her personal feelings.

But Dan Quayle and his fellow conservatives were saying something completely different. They were saying family values are part of a transcendent moral code that is binding on everyone. They were saying there are objective standards against which we can measure people's behavior.

That's the difference.

As long as you are merely expressing your own feelings, you are free to say whatever you like. But if you maintain the existence of a moral code that is objective and universal, you have committed a grave transgression against the reigning ethos of individualism.

That's why in the *TV Guide* interview Candice Bergen complained that Dan Quayle had become "arrogant," "aggressive," and "offensive." The reason is *not*, as we have seen, that she disagreed with him. She actually holds a lot of the same family values. His offense is that he actually holds these values as objective truths.

When we participate in the family values debate, we have to understand what the other side really thinks. The root of the debate runs deeper than family issues.

The real disagreement is over the very nature of truth.

THEY JUST DON'T GET IT

The War Over Family Values

The "Murphy Brown" episode came back to haunt us again. At the 1992 Emmy awards, the creator of the sitcom hailed single parents and urged them, "Don't let anyone tell you you're not a family."

Why has family values become such a disputed topic? Why were the media so quick to jump on a single line in a single speech by Dan Quayle?

The answer is that the family is at the heart of a major cultural divide in America today—a divide over the question of moral authority. It involves questions like: How do we justify saying there's only one model for the family? How can we say that some relationships are immoral?

How do we know what's right and wrong?

James Davison Hunter, in his book *Culture Wars*, says Americans hold two competing visions of moral authority. On one side is what he calls the orthodox vision. It sees institutions like the family as created by God. Moral standards are rooted in the structure of creation.

In this view, right and wrong are absolute, binding on everyone.

On the other side is what Hunter calls the progressive vision. It sees institutions like the family as a creation of human society to meet human needs. If people want to, they are free to experiment with other ways to meet those needs—other kinds of relationships.

Right and wrong are not absolute in this view, they are relative.

Once we understand these two competing visions we can make sense of the raucous debates on the talk shows and the nightly news. People who hold the orthodox view defend what we call traditional family values. People who hold the progressive view tend to reject traditional family values.

This doesn't mean all progressives are immoral or anti-family. There are plenty of progressives who live stable, caring lives, and are highly committed to their families. The point is that they have no transcendent *reason* for their commitment.

As Robert Bellah explains in his book, *Habits of the Heart*, many Americans have high ideals, but they have no transcendent principles upon which to base those ideals. Ask them *why* they are faithful to their spouses, ask them *why* they care about their kids, and all they can say is, "It feels right for me."

By the same token, they can't say why anything is wrong either. If values are what feels right to me, then I have to give *you* the freedom to do what feels right to you. Anyone who holds the orthodox vision—who says some things are right or wrong for everyone—strikes progressives as bigoted.

Francis Schaeffer used to say that Christians need to stop seeing issues in bits and pieces and start seeing the big picture. The big picture behind the family values debate is simple: Are morals absolute or are they relative? Are they God-given or do we make them up as we go along?

Christians ought to take the lead in moving the national debate away from clichés and simple sloganeering. We need to educate our neighbors on the real meaning of the "Murphy Brown" firestorm.

What we have in the family values debate is a fundamental disagreement between two world-views.

CRIMES OF FASHION

I'd Kill for That Coat

Seventeen-year-old Brenda Adams went to a party wearing a brand-new leather coat. But she didn't come back wearing the coat.

In fact, she didn't come back at all.

As Brenda was leaving the party, she was accosted by two tough-talking girls who demanded her coat. She was beaten, kicked, and dragged across the street. Then one of the girls pulled out a gun and shot her.

As Brenda lay dying, the girls ripped off her coat.

It's a tragic example of a crime wave that's hitting our cities—kids killing kids for their designer clothes. Reporters are calling them "crimes of fashion."

In some places a quarter of all armed robberies now involve clothing. In Milwaukee, an eighteen-year-old was shot for his San Francisco 49ers jacket. In Newark, a fifteen-year-old was shot by five youths who wanted his bomber jacket.

Schools are trying to control the violence by imposing stricter dress codes. The principal of a Brooklyn high school banned shearling coats and gold chains. The Detroit Board of Education imposed a new dress code after two students were killed for their Nike shoes and expensive jackets.

What's behind these bizarre armed robberies?

Since most of the violence occurs in low-income neighborhoods, it would be easy to pin the blame on poverty. Maybe these kids steal because they can't afford to buy their own designer items.

But teens who steal aren't taking just one for their own use. Police have arrested kids with four or five jackets hanging in their closets. Newark police arrested one boy with sixteen jackets.

No, the real reason for the robberies is that clothes have become potent status symbols. Wearing $150 shoes is a way of proving you're important; you're a big shot.

By the same token, stealing something is a way of striking at someone *else's* status. A Milwaukee district attorney says that the robberies are about "humiliation and power."

This is materialism run recklessly amok. Where material things define the person. Where your jacket is more important than your life.

The young people who commit these murders must be held responsible, of course. But so must society at large. In the past, families, schools, and churches worked hard to teach children moral values, self-control, and respect for others.

But today, children are more likely to be on their own. They have less supervision, less input from adults who care about them. As a result, they are falling prey to the crassest of advertising and commercialism.

They literally believe clothes make the man.

We find the same attitude among children in our wealthiest suburbs. Teachers in posh Fairfax County, Virginia, report that even first-graders are acutely conscious of which kids are wearing designer clothes to school.

On every level, the problem is the same: People whose dignity is no longer rooted in being creatures made in the image of God are searching desperately for other ways to feel important, other ways to create a sense of significance.

As Christians, we must not merely condemn, we must reach out with the only source of genuine individual dignity: that the God of the universe made you and loves you.

Kids giving up their lives for fashion need to hear that there's something much bigger to give their lives to.

Dating Etiquette
What's Behind Date Rape?

A study of junior-high students reveals some pretty startling facts about their dating etiquette. Half the youngsters said that when a man pays for a date, he has a right to kiss the woman. A fifth said that he has a right to sexual intercourse with her. Is *this* sexual liberation? When a man buys sex by buying dinner? When a concert ticket is a ticket to sex? And what if the woman thought the concert invitation was really *just* a concert invitation? A man who feels *entitled* to sex may end up using force. The result: date rape, currently one of the biggest issues on college campuses.

Date rape is a tragedy. The victim is shamed and humiliated. She becomes the butt of cruel jokes in the fraternity houses. And the authorities are likely to cover it up to protect the school's reputation.

Feminists are trying to change all that by drawing public attention to the problem. But they're ignoring the question at the heart of the issue: Why is date rape happening? Why have social restraints broken down so completely that young men feel they have a right to sexual favors—even by force?

The answer is in the old biblical principle: You reap what you sow. For years, our society has sown the seed of sexual permissiveness. Sex dominates movies, television, and popular music.

In some places a young man is handed a package of condoms in high school: a clear signal—from school authorities no less—that he's expected to be sexually active.

The old code of chivalry has been discredited. Remember the time when no man could claim to be civilized unless he showed courtesy and protectiveness toward women? Radical feminists have denounced that old code as oppressive.

But I wonder if women didn't prefer the so-called oppressive ideal of men opening doors for them to the *new* ideal some men have adopted in its place: That a real man takes whatever he can get sexually. That a real man doesn't take no for an answer.

What feminists seem unable to understand is that the loss of the older code puts women at risk. To state the obvious, there are biological differences between the sexes. It's easier to assault a woman than a man. When moral and social constraints are lifted, it's women who become more vulnerable.

Feminists say the solution to date rape is for men to respect women who say no. But that's not enough. The real problem is that sex has been stripped of its moral dimension. It's been reduced to a clash of personal desires.

The man says, "I want," and the woman says, "I don't want"—but they have no moral principles to support their decision, no common code of decency binding on them both.

It's one private will pitted against the other.

Add alcohol or drugs to the equation, and you have a classic setup for date rape.

America needs a recommitment to the idea that sex is more than a private choice. It's a moral issue. There are moral standards transcending what you or I may want at the moment.

The 1960s sowed the slogan of free sex. Today we are reaping a harvest of forced sex.

In sex, as in politics, freedom without moral restraints leads to might is right.

VIRGINS SPEAK OUT

Glamour *Magazine Discovers Chastity*

Glamour magazine made a shocking discovery: Many of its readers are virgins.

It all started when the magazine asked its readers a question: "Are there any virgins left out there?" The response took the editors by surprise: two thousand women wrote in to say that *they* were virgins—and proud of it.

The magazine summarized the responses in a March 1992 article entitled, "2,000 Virgins: They're *Not* Who You Think." In other words, they're not ugly wallflowers. They're intelligent, "with-it" young women, who are articulate, who know what they want, and who read sophisticated magazines. Like *Glamour.*

They've simply chosen not to have sex outside marriage.

Judging by their letters, it is not an easy choice to make these days. The women told stories of being teased and humiliated, accused of being prudish, and made to feel like freaks. Some women even sent in photos to prove that they're really just normal human beings.

In the face of such intense opposition, why are there still young people who stand against the current? The women who wrote in listed several good reasons.

Almost all of them listed AIDS and other sexually transmitted diseases as a good reason to remain chaste. Others said they didn't want to be pressured into sex by peer pressure and the media.

Many said that sex is too meaningful for a casual relationship. As one woman put it, "a lot of feelings, trust, and intimacy are put into a relationship once sex is involved." That's why she wants to save it for a relationship that's going to last.

Others warned that sex outside marriage loses its deep meaning. One woman told *Glamour* that sex is for expressing love— and you can't possibly love a new person every few months. Casual sex tears it out of the context of love and turns it into selfish gratification.

What's interesting is that none of the women spoke of sex as something bad or dirty. Yet the standard stereotype is that people who abstain just don't like sex very much. *Glamour* itself quoted sexologist Sol Gordon saying that saving sex for someone you love implies that sex by itself is dirty.

But the virgins who wrote in didn't express a low view of sex. On the contrary, they saw it as something intensely meaningful— so special that it should be saved for a special context: for the committed relationship of marriage.

One letter writer said, "God doesn't forbid sex before marriage because He wants to put us in a box with a list of rules and no fun." No, it's because "He wants the best for us."

That hits at the core of the issue. God's laws aren't capricious or arbitrary. They tell us who we are and what is truly best for us.

The sexual revolution is running down and people are beginning to see that sexual morals make sense after all. The old moral laws aren't just for old fogies. They're for young people, too. Even for sophisticated young women who read magazines like *Glamour*.

WHAT'S WRONG WITH CHILDREN'S RIGHTS?

Is It Really Good for Children?
A well-known Christian television show was dealing with the subject of Hillary Clinton. The tone of the show had been critical of Mrs. Clinton when one of the co-hosts spoke up: "But what about all the good things she does for children through the Children's Defense Fund?"

Well, what *about* that? Hillary Clinton has long been an ardent advocate of children's rights—and isn't that a good thing?

Well, it depends on what you mean by the term.

Most of us probably think of broad human rights, like the right to be treated honestly and fairly. But Hillary Clinton and the Children's Defense Fund are talking specifically about *legal* rights for children—rights that can be enforced by law or through the courts.

And legal rights for children would inevitably have the effect of intruding the state into family life and creating vast new government bureaucracies.

A legal right means nothing unless it can be claimed against someone. Legal rights for children will be claimed either against their parents or against the government.

In the first case, children could sue their parents over a disagreement concerning which school the children want to attend. Children's rights give minors a legal standing against their parents—treating them as mini-adults, capable of making their own decisions.

Hillary Clinton calls this "the presumption of competence"—referring to legal competence. She insists that children should have a legal right alongside their parents to make decisions about such issues as whether to attend school, whether to get a job, and whether to have an abortion.

This idea is more radical than it sounds, warns columnist Paul Gigot in the *Wall Street Journal.* If adopted by the Supreme Court, "the theory would give the state a wedge to pry into family decisions," Gigot says. "It's just what our lawsuit-happy society needs: Kids suing Dad over a job at McDonald's."

The other side of children's rights is that it would greatly expand state bureaucracy. Consider: If a child has a legal right to quality day care, against whom can that right be claimed? Not the parents this time, but the government. It is merely an inverse way of saying the government has a duty to provide day care. That's why Hillary Clinton, as chairman of the Children's Defense Fund, worked passionately for federally funded day care.

A child's right becomes a bureaucrat's duty.

The election of Bill Clinton to the presidency has brought Hillary Clinton to the public eye and has raised an issue that will be with us for a long time: namely, what is the role of government in the lives of children?

Christians ought to be very cautious of anyone who recommends decreasing the role of parents and increasing the role of the state in family life. God created the family as the basic unit of society and planned that truth would be passed from parents to children, from generation to generation.

Children's rights theory claims to promote the welfare of children. But in reality it throws children into the arms of state professionals—who may be filled with big ideas but empty of the bonds of family love.

KIDDIE DIVORCE

Should Children Divorce Their Parents?

America's divorce rate is a national scandal—but it could soon get much worse. If children's rights groups have their way, divorce will go beyond husbands and wives...to include the kids.

In a groundbreaking decision, a Florida judge ruled that an eleven-year-old boy named Gregory had the right to divorce his parents. Gregory charged his parents with abuse and neglect and wanted to be adopted by his foster parents.

Now obviously a child should not have to remain in an abusive home. But remedies for cases like that are already available. Our legal system allows a state-appointed guardian or child welfare agency to petition for a change of custody.

Gregory's case could have gone through the normal channels. Instead, the judge decided to create a *new* right out of thin air. For perhaps the first time in our nation's history, a child was given legal standing to divorce his parents.

Children's rights advocates were ecstatic. One lawyer said the decision strikes down what he called "the old paternalistic mumbo-jumbo that says children have no rights."

But hold it a minute. No one ever said children have no rights. It's illegal to murder children—which means they have a right to life. It's illegal to kidnap children—so they have a right to liberty. It's illegal to steal from children—so they have a right to property.

But there's a big difference between universal rights like these and procedural rights, like voting or representing yourself in court. Procedural rights are limited to adults who are mature enough to understand the law. Children are traditionally represented by parents or guardians, a system that protects them from direct legal accountability.

What children's rights advocates want to do is rip away that protection and give them the same responsibilities as adults. Karen Adams of the National Child Rights Alliance says that she'd like to see kids have the right to go to court to decide things for themselves as soon as they learn how to talk. "We've had…children as young as three years old saying, 'I don't want to live here anymore,'" Adams says. In her ideal world, tots could sue in court before they're even big enough to cross the street by themselves.

The rhetoric of liberation leads straight to litigation.

Of course, practically speaking, kids aren't knowledgeable

enough to claim legal rights on their own. If they don't depend on their parents to represent them, they'll turn to other people—like lawyers and social workers.

As a result, the real effect of so-called children's rights is to take power away from parents and give it to outside professionals.

What's behind children's rights is a mentality that sees family bonds as narrow and constricting and views the state as a tool for liberating people from those bonds.

It's the Enlightenment worship of individual autonomy—extended down to youngsters.

THE NEW PRIVACY RIGHT

Now It's for Kids, Too
The right to privacy.

It's not mentioned anywhere in the Constitution, but in 1973 the Supreme Court decided it existed anyway—and that it guaranteed the right to abortion.

But privacy may soon be used to guarantee a whole slew of other rights.

Take a recent example. In Florida, a circuit judge threw out charges against two young men for violating the state's statutory rape law. Florida law makes it illegal to engage in sexual relations with a girl below the age of sixteen—whether she consents or not.

The idea is that some actions are so significant that young teens and adolescents shouldn't even be asked to consent to them before they're mature enough to understand the consequences.

Nevertheless, the judge threw the case out.

On what grounds? On the right to privacy, enshrined in Florida's state constitution.

The judge argued that if the right to privacy allows minors to choose whether to have an *abortion* without consulting their parents, then surely it must also allow them to choose whether to have sexual relations.

Now most of us thought it was bad enough for the state to

intrude into the relationship between parents and children on the issue of abortion. But it turns out abortion was just the wedge that would pry open a floodgate for the whole so-called children's rights agenda.

The judge's ruling was one step in that direction. Consider: If abortion is interpreted to guarantee children the right to sexual relations, where does the reasoning stop? Can they make their own decisions about attending school? Guess that gets rid of compulsory education laws. Can they make their own decisions about whether to work? Guess that gets rid of child labor laws.

And how far down the age scale does this privacy principle extend? What about ten-year-olds? Or five-year-olds?

Behind the judge's decision is a theory that denies the reality of developmental stages in childhood and adolescence that warrant adult protection. The theory was expressed by Hillary Clinton, an advocate of children's rights, in an article that shrugged off the idea of adolescence as sheer "invention." And it was expressed in another recent court case, where a judge said that there's nothing "magic" that happens to kids when they reach "the age of maturity."

Well, I don't know if maturity is "magic," but as any parent knows, it's real. There are genuine developmental differences between a six-year-old, a twelve-year-old, and an eighteen-year-old. It's only common sense to acknowledge those differences in law—by placing young children under their parents' protection.

By denying those differences, children's rights advocates are busy removing parental protection. The statutory rape ruling is just one example. The ACLU tipped its hand when it praised the ruling as one step toward giving children the same rights as adults.

The case gives us a glimpse into the kind of world that children's rights folks really want: a world without parental authority and without childhood innocence.

BEATING UP ON DAD

Images of Fathers in Children's Literature

It looks like a charming children's story—three little bears on a scouting escapade. But who's this? Papa Bear is coming along. And at every step of the way, Papa makes a complete fool of himself. If Papa suggests the direction to take, the path is sure to end up in a swamp. If he makes the campfire stew, it's sure to taste awful. Just what is this book teaching kids about fathers?

The story I just described is from the highly popular Berenstain Bears series. In several of the books, Papa Bear is portrayed as a bumbling oaf. The sensible one in the family is Mama Bear.

In the story on junk food, Papa is the worst offender. It's Mama who enforces the switch to a healthy diet. In the story on manners, again, Papa is the worst offender. It's Mama who enforces politeness.

Isn't there anything Papa does best? Well, yes, he's given one distinction. In a book on fitness, the children outdo Papa on every skill except one: Sister Bear can run the fastest, Brother Bear can jump the farthest, but when the exercise session is over, Papa Bear can sleep the longest.

Ha, ha. Let's all have a good laugh at Papa's expense.

This treatment of fathers is, sad to say, not the exception but the rule in children's books. In a recent issue of *Newsweek* a young father complains that he has a terrible time finding books for his children that show fathers in a positive light.

Or finding books that even show fathers at all. Remember Babar the elephant? When Babar's mother is killed by a hunter, the baby elephant is pronounced an orphan. But wait a minute: Why is he an orphan? Doesn't he have a father? Doesn't his father care?

The same bias against dads carries over into books for teens. A survey of contemporary teen literature found that the majority portray mother-headed families.

Even when fathers are part of the story, they're much more likely than mothers to be cruel and abusive. The few times fathers are portrayed as good, they're nice but weak: They stand aside with a smile and let the teenagers decide for themselves what to do.

What will happen to a society where children's imaginations are filled with images of fathers who are oafs and fools? And it's no good saying this is all "just" fiction, the way people said several years ago about Murphy Brown. When children read story upon story with absent or abusive fathers, that can't help but shape their expectations.

Psychologists recognize the emotional impact of books—so much so that there's even a branch of counseling today called "bibliotherapy," which uses storybooks to change children's attitudes.

And if stories have the power to do good, then clearly they have the power to do harm.

That's why the women's movement has worked so hard to change the image of women in children's books. And the civil rights movement has worked to root out negative images of black people.

Maybe it's time to start a movement for fathers.

FATHER HUNGER

The Men's Movement

Seven hundred men gathered in 1992 in Austin, Texas, to squat around campfires, pound drums, and howl and sweat together. It was the First International Men's Conference, and participants were hoping to rediscover their true manhood.

Yes, just as the sixties gave birth to the women's movement, so the nineties promise to give birth to a movement for men.

It's easy to poke fun at the drums and the feathers. Yet two books on the subject—*Iron John* and *Fire in the Belly*—have been on the *New York Times* bestseller list for nearly two years.

Obviously, underneath the silly stuff, the movement is touching some kind of nerve. What is it?

Robert Bly, author of *Iron John*, says that American men suffer from "fatherlessness"—boys growing up without their fathers. If you think back to colonial times, life was much different. Fathers worked alongside their sons on farms and in family industries, passing on the skills *their* fathers taught them. The Industrial Revolution changed all that. It tore fathers out of the home to work in factories and offices. For the first time in history, women became the primary parents.

Today, boys spend most of their growing years around women—with their mothers at home and with female teachers at school and at Sunday school. They grow up with only the haziest notion of what their fathers do all day.

According to the Family Research Council, the average father spends only eight minutes a day in direct conversation with his children. In families where the mother works, too, it drops to four minutes.

No wonder many boys suffer from what Robert Bly calls "father hunger"—a longing for a man's love, an insecure sense of masculine identity.

Signs of the malaise were everywhere at the First International Men's Conference. In workshops men openly wept and railed against fathers who had neglected or abandoned them. Grown men talked of the need for father figures to overcome the pain they still carried inside.

Well, like most secular movements, the men's movement may pinpoint some valid problems, but its solutions are woefully inadequate. You don't mend a wound in the heart by squatting in tents and banging on drums.

The real solution is found in Psalm 27:10—"My father and my mother have forsaken me, but the Lord will take me up." It is the Lord who is a Father to the fatherless. He can heal emotional wounds and give the kind of love the human heart longs for.

Over the next several years, the problem of fatherless men is likely to grow worse. We're just beginning to see the fallout from the rise in divorce rates since the sixties. Only a few years after a divorce, most fathers lose contact with their children.

In addition, there's been an increase in children who never *had* contact with their fathers—whose parents never married. Boys growing up yesterday may have suffered neglect from fathers who were too busy, but many boys growing up today suffer from having no father at all.

The church needs to be praying and planning how it will minister to these fatherless men—Big Brother programs, mentoring relationships, and classes to teach fathering skills.

Reach out to young men *before* they head for the hills and the tom-toms. Point them toward the heavenly Father—the only person who can really satisfy their "father hunger."

DADDY, COME HOME

The Epidemic of Absent Fathers

Ask a typical government bureaucrat what the problems facing our nation are, and you're likely to hear a lot of abstract talk about economic trends and trade deficits.

But ask Luis Sullivan, secretary of the Department of Health and Human Services under the Bush administration, and he'll tell you that the greatest challenge of our generation is the flight of men from family life.

Since the 1960s, America has seen a staggering increase in broken families. Liberal social scientists don't like to use phrases like "broken families"; they glibly describe them in neutral terms like "new family forms" and "single-parent homes."

But in the eyes of a child, what's nearly always happening is the loss of a father.

And statistics show that the results of that loss are devastating. While the national poverty rate is 6 percent, the poverty rate for female-headed households is 30 percent. Among black female-headed households, it jumps to 50 percent.

The blunt fact is that poverty is not going to be eradicated from our black communities so long as nearly 70 percent of black children are born out of wedlock.

And with no-fault divorce, poverty is rapidly making inroads into the middle class as well. Half of all new welfare recipients are recently divorced women and their children. Today the most reliable indicator of whether a child is poor is whether or not he lives in an intact family.

But a missing father means much more than a missing paycheck. A father's love and discipline are crucial to character formation. And for children growing up without that love, the statistics are grim.

Fatherless children display more antisocial behavior, do worse in school, and are twice as likely to drop out than children from intact families. They are more likely to use drugs and become sexually active at an early age. More than half the teenagers who have attempted suicide live in single-parent homes.

Most children who run away from home are leaving fatherless homes. And approximately 70 percent of juveniles who end up in long-term correctional facilities grew up without a father at home.

Even health rates are affected. A recent study by the Department of Health and Human Services found that after controlling for age, sex, race, and socioeconomic status, children from broken families are twenty to forty times more likely to suffer health problems than children living with both parents.

The numbers are overwhelming. Our nation can no longer afford to be morally neutral about family forms. For the sake of our children, we must begin to design social policies that support and encourage intact families.

Which is to say, we need programs that encourage *men* to take their family responsibilities more seriously.

Most of our national dialogue on family issues, most of our parenting classes, most of our social supports for parents focus on mothers. But it is not women who are abandoning or neglecting their children, says Secretary Sullivan. It is men.

The time has come to shift our attention to the issue of male responsibility and the indispensable role fathers play in family life.

There's a reason God created the family the way He did. Children need fathers as well as mothers in order to thrive. And even more important, in order to learn to trust God as their *heavenly* Father.

GRANNY DUMPING

The Costs of Family Breakdown

In a hospital in Tampa, Florida, an elderly woman was dropped off—and never picked up again. She was found at the door of the emergency room, slumped in her wheelchair. A note pinned to her purse read, "She's sick. Please take care of her."

When the hospital staff looked around for the woman's family, all they saw was a pair of taillights disappearing into the distance.

This is just one story in a growing trend that's been dubbed "granny dumping." Staff at Tampa General Hospital say that only a few years ago they almost never saw elderly people abandoned on their doorstep. Now, they say, it happens two or three times a week.

What we're seeing here is a coming together of demographics and moral breakdown.

America's population is aging, and the baby boom generation is moving up the age curve. Our birthrate has gone down, and our survival rate has gone up. The result is an expanding population of elderly people—with a shrinking base of younger people to care for them.

That in itself would have produced a tremendous strain on the younger generation trying to care for aging relatives. But making things worse is a flight from family responsibilities that has plagued American society since the 1960s.

For example, ever since the sixties larger numbers of people are remaining single or *becoming* single again through divorce or separation. These people have a harder time caring for aging parents, just as they have a harder time caring for young children.

The fact is it takes two people to care for dependents—one to earn an income, another to give care and nurture. Yet one study found that nearly half the people who care for elderly relatives today are single.

Another factor making it harder to care for the elderly is an increase in the number of families that are raising children at the same time. One study found that four out of five families caring for elderly parents still have children under sixteen years of age living at home. Demographers call this group the "sandwich generation"—squeezed between caring for two kinds of dependents at the same time.

This, too, is often a result of the flight from family. For many years the cultural message to young women has been that having a career is more important than having a family. As a result, women began putting off childbearing. Today the average age of childbearing is in the low-to mid-thirties, much older than a generation ago.

Many of these late families end up taking care of baby and granny at the same time.

Late families can also be the result of divorce and remarriage. It's not unusual today for parents to have a set of teenagers and a set of toddlers from a second marriage. The second-time-around family is prime for becoming part of the sandwich generation.

Americans like to think it's their own business whether they marry, whether they have children, and whether they divorce. But private choices always have public consequences.

The family is God's basic unit for health, education, and welfare. When people make choices that weaken the family, it threatens the health, the education, and the welfare of our entire society—leaving some people out in the cold.

Maybe out on a hospital driveway.

THE REVOLT AGAINST FEMINISM
Susan Faludi's Backlash

A new word has entered the political vocabulary. It's "backlash" and it's been popularized in a book entitled *Backlash: The Undeclared War Against American Women.*

The most potent weapon in this "undeclared war," says the author, Susan Faludi, is the myth that feminism has failed. As Faludi sees it, everywhere—from Hollywood to Madison Avenue to the nightly news—people are conspiring to make women believe that feminism is dead, conspiring to drive women out of the workplace and back into the kitchen.

Well, Faludi is right in saying there's a trend against feminism—but her interpretation of this trend is dead wrong.

It is *women* who are moving away from ideological feminism. They are rethinking the knee-jerk commitment to outside careers. A poll by *Time* and CNN found that 63 percent of women today do not consider themselves feminists.

Faludi would have us think this is all due to an ugly, coercive backlash, concocted by reactionary forces to keep women subordinate. Faludi, who is not married and has never had any children, can't conceive that intelligent, adult women would actually choose to spend a major portion of their lives caring for children and creating a rich family life.

It *must* be some outside conspiracy.

But the idea of backlash is contradicted by the enormous attention Faludi's own book is getting—culminating in a cover story in *Time* magazine.

No signs of a backlash there.

The truth is that the rejection of feminism is no conspiracy being foisted upon women. It's a change welling up from within the minds and hearts of women themselves.

And it's happening even within the feminist movement itself. Betty Friedan, who helped launch the movement with her book *The Feminist Mistique,* later wrote *The Second Stage,* where she worried that feminists had denied the importance of family life. Germaine Greer, who condemned marriage and motherhood in her book *The Female Eunuch,* later wrote *Sex and Destiny,* which celebrated children and family.

Reporter and novelist Sally Quinn rocked the readership of the *Washington Post* with a biting critique of feminism.

Clearly, it's not just so-called reactionaries who are critical of feminism. Even women weaned on feminist ideology are rethinking their views.

What's really happening is quite simple: The baby boomers are having babies and raising families of their own.

And that's changing their values and perspectives.

Listen to the poignant story told by feminist Erica Jong. Shortly after she had her first baby, Jong was invited to a poetry reading. It was her first public appearance after giving birth, and Jong decided to read several poems expressing the deep feelings she experienced in becoming a mother.

An audience of radical feminists booed her off the stage. Jong was devastated. Today she writes articles on the failure of feminism—rooted, she says, in its unwillingness to recognize the central fact in the lives of 90 percent of American women: the fact that they have children and that they resent being made to feel guilty about it.

So Faludi is wrong. There is no outside conspiracy. Just a spontaneous change as a generation of men and women, made in the image of God, grow up and discover the normal joys of family and children.

COMING HOME

The New Traditional Mother

The group of women meeting in the living room of a Washington, D.C., home was remarkably diverse. The only thing that seemed to unite them was a common commitment to being home with their young children.

On one side of the room were the traditionalists. Crisply coifed and conservatively dressed, they represented a national Christian organization called Home by Choice.

Then there were the countercultural types: no makeup, long hair, babies toted in slings across their shoulders. These women represented Mothers at Home, one of the country's first advocacy groups for mothers.

Across the room sat a group of highly professional women—women who had agonized over leaving well-paying, successful careers when they decided to stay home with their children. They formed a group called Mothers First.

Then there were women from a group called Lawyers at Home, there being enough lawyers in Washington to form a group just for themselves. These women had a tough look about them and spoke in the aggressive manner of the courtroom lawyer. But they, too, had come to support mothers who want to take time out from their careers to raise their own children.

What drew this amazingly diverse group of women together was the sense that the tide is changing. For the first time in decades, there is a renewed respect for mothers who choose to stay home.

After the rise of militant feminism in the sixties, many women felt that being a mother and a homemaker was a trivial job, second best—that they really should be doing something better with their talents.

Lonna Wilkinson, a dancer and choreographer, describes the feeling well. "For women of my generation," she says, "motherhood really got a bum rap." There was a sense that there were more important things to do in life than be a mother.

But women still feel the age-old tug to nurture new life. Last year, the annual number of births in America jumped to 4 million for the first time since the end of the postwar baby boom. This was a steep increase in the number of births, and it appears to have taken place among both younger women and older women, who had postponed childbearing.

Motherhood is becoming popular again.

The change set in when women who had delayed childbearing couldn't put it off any longer and began having children.

They discovered that having a baby was far more fulfilling than they'd been led to believe.

Carlie Dixon was thirty-five when she became pregnant with her first child. Carlie had practiced law for nine years and was a partner in a Washington, D.C., law firm. She fully intended to return to work after the birth of her child. But when her child was placed in her arms, her whole value system turned upside down.

"I was completely unprepared for the emotional attachment I would have with this child," Carlie says. "I didn't realize how much I would want to spend time with him."

Carlie is not alone. An article in *U.S. News & World Report* noted that for the first time in decades there has been a slight but statistically significant drop in the number of mothers in the work force.

More women are staying home—and enjoying it more. A 1989 survey by the Roper Organization found that 66 percent of women described having children as "very satisfying." Only 35 percent described their jobs in the same terms.

Yes, after decades of getting a "bum rap," to use Lonna Wilkinson's phrase, motherhood is coming back into its own.

FAMILY TIME FAMINE

Giving Parents More Time

American families are spending less time together than ever, says a well-known sociologist. She calls it the "family time famine." Statistics show that today's parents spend 40 percent less time with their children than their parents did.

That's a staggering decrease in adult investment in children.

The good news is that some parents are trying to reverse the trend. A story in the *Washington Post* announced that fast-track professionals are slowing down. They're exploring things like part-time work and flexible schedules to create more family time.

Lynn Myers is a pediatrician who began working part time when her first son was born. Today her children are older, but she still restricts her work to school hours, so she can help with homework or drive to soccer practice.

Driving a kid to soccer may not sound as glamorous as working in a prestigious medical practice. But it can be much more important. Lynn Myers says, "I find my kids share a lot of their successes and hurts" during that time together.

Today one of the fastest-growing options is home-based work, integrating family and work. Caroline Hull is a computer specialist who started her own business at home when her children were born. Jeannie Herbert is a nurse who holds childbirth education classes in her home.

But it isn't just women who are working to solve the family time famine. Bob Hamrin was economic adviser to a national political figure when he decided he wanted more time with his growing family. Bob left a promising political career to start a home-based consulting firm, taking time off to attend a child's school function or sports event.

Stepping off the fast track when your children are young isn't easy. As I think back on my own life, my biggest regret is not spending more time with my kids.

Really making family the top priority means standing against a culture where materialism and workaholism are rampant. It means realizing you may not advance as fast in your career as some of your colleagues—at least for a few years. It means being willing to accept a lower standard of living.

Call it the "Parent Penalty."

In today's high-powered career world, parents who really invest in family life pay the Parent Penalty. But the trade-off is knowing you're doing the right thing for your children, giving them the emotional security they'll draw on for the rest of their lives.

There's a professional trade-off, too. People who enjoy a healthy family life make better workers. The Association for Part-Time Professionals says part-time workers invest more productive efforts into the hours they do spend on the job.

Good parents make good workers.

Unfortunately, it's not always easy to persuade businesses and corporations of that. Even Christian ministries can fall into the trap of workaholism. In one Christian ministry, workers were told that if a job could be done in a normal forty-hour week, then management hadn't put enough workload into the position.

But we should expect Christian businesses and ministries, of all people, to uphold the importance of the family. They should be taking the lead in creating family-friendly work strategies: things like part-time positions, flexible hours, and home-based work.

Encouraging a healthy family life is not only a biblical principle. It also happens to be good business.

STRUGGLING

WITH

DEATH

BILLY GRAHAM

Billy Graham
World-renowned evangelist
Special advisor to six U.S. presidents
Author of bestselling books

Dr. Donald Grey Barnhouse was one of America's great preachers. His first wife died from cancer when she was in her thirties, leaving three children under the age of twelve. Barnhouse chose to preach the funeral sermon himself. What does a father tell his motherless children at a time like this?

On his way to the service, he was driving with his little family when a large truck passed them on the highway, casting a shadow over their car. Barnhouse turned to his oldest daughter who was staring disconsolately out the window, and asked, "Tell me, sweetheart, would you rather be run over by that truck or its shadow?"

The little girl looked curiously at her father and said, "By the shadow, I guess. It can't hurt you."

Dr. Barnhouse said quietly to the three children, "Your mother has not been overrun by death, but by the shadow of death. That is nothing to fear." At the funeral he used the text from the Twenty-third Psalm, which so eloquently expresses this truth. That illustration from Dr. Barnhouse's own experience has been used by countless preachers to help other families face their fear of death.

Many people say they do not fear death, but the *process* of dying. It's not the destination, but the trip that they dread.

John Newton, a one-time slave trader, was converted and became a great preacher and hymn writer in the Church of England. Two years before his death, in 1807, he was so weak that he could hardly stand in his pulpit; someone had to support him as he preached. Shortly before he died, when he was confined to his room and unable to move, he told a friend, "I am like a person going on a journey in a stagecoach, who expects its arrival every hour and is frequently looking out of the window for it....I am packed and sealed, and ready for the post."[1]

You may have heard of Newton; he wrote some words which are sung around the world: "Amazing grace, how sweet the sound."

THE DANGERS OF DENIAL

Whether our last trip is by stagecoach, slow and arduous, or by jet, swift and smooth, the journey through the valley eventually comes to a stop. How should we travel, and how can we help the ones we love along the way?

As Christians we are constantly bombarded with attitudes and values which are contrary to biblical teaching. Even though the subject of death has come out of the closet, the denial of one's own mortality is instinctive in most of us. No matter how well we take care of ourselves, there may come a time when we face a severe health problem. Sometimes we are not given a choice about our physical or mental condition. How can we live in a basically non-Christian culture and cope with the despair that may come when death seems near?

In her inimitable bravado, Katherine Hepburn said, "I think we're finally at a point where we've learned to see death with a sense of humor. I have to. When you're my age, it's as if you're a car. First a tire blows, and you get that fixed. Then a headlight goes, and you get that fixed. And then one day, you drive into a shop, and the man says, 'Sorry, Miss, they don't have this make anymore.'"[2]

But a time comes when the humor becomes deadly serious. Anyone who is told he has a fatal illness cannot just laugh it off. The first reaction is, "You must be wrong." "Not me." Bad news is all too frequently met, first, with disbelief.

Denial can be very dangerous. A prominent urologist endured severe lower back pains over a long period of time; although he had diagnosed patients with similar conditions, he refused to get treatment until his own condition was beyond hope of a medical cure. He did not want to hear the bad news, so he opted for no news.

Dr. Ruth Kopp, a Christian doctor specializing in clinical oncology, has had many years of experience with terminally ill patients. She wrote: "The first important effect of denial I've seen in my relationship with patients is that it produces a partial deafness. Although the hospital staff told Jesse (the patient) that he had widespread, inoperable cancer, he was deaf to much of what he had heard. He was not unique in that respect!"[3] A terminally ill patient may reject what he has heard, and then deny the need for treatment. Some will listen to the doctor's diagnosis and then begin a round of searching for other doctors who will give them happier news. Of course, there is nothing wrong with getting other qualified opinions; this should not be considered denial. Others look for unorthodox methods and spend time and money for temporary, often fraudulent, cures for their symptoms instead of facing the reality of their condition.

Denial isn't necessarily a sign of weakness, but a normal emotion that needs to be voiced. Sometimes it can serve as a protective mechanism to shield a person from threatening situations before the individual is emotionally ready to handle them. If we persist in denial, however, we are cutting ourselves off from the help we need—from others and from God.

The prophet Jeremiah said, "You can't heal a wound by say-ing it's not there" (Jeremiah 6:14, LB). And yet we want to ignore a diagnosis about our physical state if it is unpleasant.

Chaplain Phil Manly tells a story that illustrates the force that denial can play in masking the truth. A badly burned baby was admitted to the USC Medical Center burn ward in Los Angeles. The mother was with the baby when the child died. The next day the nurse on the ward received a call from the mother asking how her baby was and what time she could visit. The nurse and Chap-lain Manly were able to bring her lovingly to accept the reality of her baby's death.

Jesus had a difficult time with the attitude of denial in His dis-ciples. He told them repeatedly that He would be betrayed and crucified, but they refused to listen. Peter even rebuked Him for saying that He was going to be killed and after three days rise again: "From that time on Jesus began to explain to his disciples that he must go to Jerusalem and suffer many things at the hands of the elders, chief priests and teachers of the law, and that he must be killed and on the third day be raised to life. Peter took him aside and began to rebuke him. 'Never, Lord!' he said. 'This shall never happen to you!'" (Matthew 16:21–22, NIV).

Peter knew Jesus told the truth, but he did not want to hear it.

WHEN TRUTH HURTS—OR HEALS

The Bible tells us to "speak the truth in love," and yet there are times when the truth seems so harsh that we play games. One way to respond when a terminally ill person is in the denial stage is to join him in the ostrich attitude. But Dr. Ruth Kopp warns, "If your response is behavior that is harmful to the individual, it is inap-propriate." Most people can't face the fact of their own deaths twenty-four hours a day, and need to pretend, at least for a while, that the situation may be just a bad dream.

We may respond to someone's denial by avoiding it. Many people who have been told they have just a few weeks or months left have lived to laugh at the diagnosis years later. A Christian may have complete confidence that God has healed him or her, despite medical reports to the contrary. A realistic answer, given with gentleness and love, might be, "We know that God can heal, and He does. But we don't know what He has in store for you or for me. Let's trust the doctors for treatment, and continue to pray for healing, asking for God's will." One doctor said he used the "wait and see" response whenever a terminally ill person said that God had healed him or her. If He hasn't then they will face that reality later.

No One Wins

Some types of denial can be dangerous for the patient and loved ones. I refer specifically to the "Let's Spare Them" game. The patient knows he or she is terminally ill. There are important things such a person wants to say to his wife and children, but he is afraid they cannot accept the fact that he may soon die, so he spares them any painful conversations. His wife, knowing her husband's time is short, wants to keep the atmosphere cheerful, so she doesn't ask the questions she needs to ask about the family and finances that are a burden on her heart. His family would like to tell him some of the things they never got around to saying when he was well, but they're afraid to upset him. Everyone plays the game, and no one is a winner.

What if, instead, dying people were urged to express themselves and talk openly about their illness? And what if the loved ones listened to such concerns, instead of ignoring them? Nothing soothes loneliness or depression as much as being able to talk about those fears and concerns.

Job's Friends: Who Needs Enemies?

Job was afflicted with so many physical and emotional problems that his name is always associated with suffering. His wealth was taken from him and his sons and daughters were crushed when a great wind demolished the house where they were dining. Job was struck with terrible boils from head to foot. His wife and brothers shunned him and children ran from the sight of him. Those who loved him turned against him. He became a joke among the people who had once respected him.

Along came those "well-meaning friends" who tried to explain the cause of his pain. One "friend" told him he was being punished by God less than he deserved. Another argued if he had been pure and good, God would hear his prayers and answer him.

In various modern guises, many of "Job's friends" are still among us today. There is nothing more dangerous than a half-truth, so let's examine what the Bible says about the sickness, disease, and pain which usually precede all but sudden, accidental deaths.

We know that when God created Adam and Eve, they were holy and healthy. They were created in His perfect image and were to remain perfect human specimens. More than that, they were not meant to experience death. But Satan ruined these two divine masterpieces, and as a result of their decision to disobey God, sin, sickness, and death entered paradise. So, human sin was the first cause of sickness and death. Since that moment in the Garden of Eden, pain and death have been the heritage of the entire human race. "...sin entered the world through one man, and death through sin, and in this way death came to all men, because all sinned..." (Romans 5:12, NIV).

Even the strain of Christian service can result in sickness. Daniel was a devoted servant of the Lord, and when he saw a vision of things to come, he fainted and was ill for many days (Daniel 8:26–27).

The apostle Paul likewise experienced frequent bouts of illness and physical weakness. He recalled to the Corinthians, "I came to you in weakness..." (1 Corinthians 2:3, NIV). He prayed also that God would take his problem away: "...there was given me a thorn in my flesh, a messenger of Satan, to torment me. Three times I pleaded with the Lord to take it away from me. But he said to me, 'My grace is sufficient for you, for my power is made perfect in weakness.' Therefore I will boast all the more gladly about my weaknesses, so that Christ's power may rest on me. That is why, for Christ's sake, I delight in weaknesses, in insults, in hardships, in persecutions, in difficulties. For when I am weak, then I am strong" (2 Corinthians 12:7b–10, NIV). I have known many Christian workers who have risked their lives and their health in serving the Lord, although I have known others whose ministries would have lasted longer if they had taken better care of themselves and learned to relax.

A leading cause of sickness today is our high-pressure lifestyle. Heart disease, ulcers, and some types of cancer often may be attributable to our ambitious pursuits and reckless living. We know that neglecting our need for good diet, rest, and good mental habits can lead to serious physical problems. The Bible says, "My people are destroyed from lack of knowledge" (Hosea 4:6, NIV).

We cannot always know or understand God's purpose in allowing us to endure physical or mental trials. I must admit that when I see someone suffer who has devoted his life to the Lord and has led an exemplary life, I find it difficult to understand. Nevertheless, we know we can trust God and His love, even when we do not understand.

My friend of many years, the late Herbert Lockyer, in his book, *All the Promises of the Bible,* illuminates some of his discoveries from the Bible concerning the purposes of sickness.[4]

One purpose is to teach us God's laws. The psalmist said, "It was good for me to be afflicted so that I might learn your decrees" (Psalm 119:71, NIV).

Another purpose of sickness and suffering is to perfect the person who sins. It's the idea that God will pull us up short to strengthen us for His purpose. "And the God of all grace, who called you to his eternal glory in Christ, after you have suffered a little while, will himself restore you and make you strong, firm and steadfast" (1 Peter 5:10, NIV).

Suffering is also meant to prepare us for a coming glory. Peter writes, "Dear friends, do not be surprised at the painful trial you are suffering, as though something strange were happening to you. But rejoice that you participate in the sufferings of Christ, so that you may be overjoyed when his glory is revealed" (Peter 4:12–13, NIV).

Also, suffering equips us to comfort others "...so that we can comfort those in any trouble with the comfort we ourselves have received from God" (2 Corinthians 1:4, NIV).

God doesn't comfort us to make us comfortable, but to make us comforters.

In addition, suffering can give us opportunities to witness. The world is a gigantic hospital; nowhere is there a greater chance to see the peace and joy of the Lord than when the journey through the valley is the darkest.

Gene and Helen Poole were Christians who had been married for sixty-five years. When Helen was in the final weeks of her life, unable to move or speak, it was the witness of her faithful husband, spending all day beside her bed in his wheelchair, that touched the lives of the staff and visitors at the convalescent home.

Perhaps you are going through a period of suffering right now. It may be because of some physical illness which has afflicted you, or it may be because of a broken relationship, a financial difficulty, or some other reason. What is your reaction to it? Are you resentful and bitter, demanding that God change your situation or lashing out at those around you for what you consider unjust treatment? Or have you yielded your life—including your suffering—to Christ and asked Him to work for His glory through your suffering, even if you do not fully understand it?

When the word came of the illness of Lazarus (who would die

and then be raised from the dead by Jesus), Jesus declared, "This sickness will not end in death. No, it is for God's glory so that God's Son may be glorified through it" (John 11:4, NIV). The same could be said of much of our suffering, as we seek God's will and strength.

The Bible warns that bitterness never solves anything, but only hurts both us and those around us: "See to it...that no bitter root grows up to cause trouble and defile many" (Hebrews 12:15, NIV). It also promises us that God can bring a harvest of good in our lives through our suffering, if we will let Him. "No discipline seems pleasant at the time, but painful. Later on, however, it produces a harvest of righteousness and peace for those who have been trained by it" (Hebrews 12:11, NIV).

William W. Kinsley has written, "Just as soon as we turn toward Him with loving confidence, and say, 'Thy will be done,' whatever chills or cripples or enslaves our spirits, clogs their powers, or hinders their development, melts away in the sunshine of His sympathy. He does not free us from the pain, but from its power."

Yes, God is with us in the midst of our suffering, and He can bless us in ways we could never have imagined. Lay your burden of suffering at the feet of Christ—who suffered on the cross for you—and ask Him to help you not only bear it but experience His victory and peace in the midst of it.

DO WE GO THROUGH STAGES?

Elisabeth Kübler-Ross was one of the first secular psychologists to observe that there are five stages that patients and their loved ones may go through in the dying process. Most people in the medical and psychological fields agree that a person doesn't march through the five stages of denial, anger, bargaining, depression, and acceptance like a programmed robot. These stages may coexist, be reversed, or be skipped, but the pattern is common in many sufferers.

Marian Holten cared for terminally ill patients for more that forty years and had many experiences seeing her patients through the valley. She had been a student nurse in the 1940s when her first assignment was to sit with a dying, comatose patient. She said those were the days when there was more personal than machine care. She pulled up a chair by the bedside, prepared for a long, tedious vigil. Suddenly she was startled when her patient, who had been unable to move or speak for weeks, opened his eyes, sat up in bed and looked around. A beautiful expression came over his face, and then he fell back on his pillow, dead.

From that time on, Marian asked to be assigned to the terminally ill. She wanted to know more about the dying experience, what happened at the moment of death, and how to help her patients through those final hours.

Denial is so strong that patients will insist they are going to do things they are incapable of doing. Marian told of a young girl who was in the last stages of acute leukemia and kept insisting that she was going to Canada. How do caring people respond when they know the desire cannot be carried our? We do not need to lie, but we must be supportive. Marian taught her student nurses to make a statement which was positive. She would say, "I can see that's something you are happy about. Tell me about Canada. Is it someplace you've always wanted to go?" Taking someone's mind off his or her illness, without supporting his or her denial, is the honest way.

When my mother was in her final days, Rose Adams would get her dressed to go out, even when she knew Mother would not be able to go. It was a game, but it made Mother happy, and that was the most important thing.

DENIAL THROUGH ANGER AND INDIFFERENCE

Anger is another very human response from those who are very ill. One patient became so angry that when the nurse came in to take his temperature in the morning, he shouted at her, "Get out of here, I can't stand your face." Marian Holten remembered another time when a patient threw a full urinal at her. How can caring people handle other people's anger? One way is with humor. Later Marian who was on the receiving end of the outburst poked her head cautiously in the door and said, "Hey, is it okay to come in now?" He laughed, realizing how unreasonably hard he had been on her, and soon they were friends.

Another type of denial is to ignore those we think are past understanding. We should never assume that people do not hear what we are saying. Among the "living dead" are those who are very much alive. Nurses report that family members, and even hospital personnel talk around a comatose patient as if he or she were already dead. At first all the family members come to the bedside of their dying loved one. Then they begin to return to their other activities and, just when the patient needs them the most, there is no one around. "It's taking him so long to die," someone says in his presence; or, "I just wish the Lord would take him and get it over with."

One nurse told how she talked quietly and encouragingly to her patient all the time she was caring for his needs, even though the doctors said he didn't know anything that was happening. He miraculously came out of his coma and upon hearing the voice of this nurse said, "Oh, you're the one who talked to me."

DENIAL THROUGH BARGAINING

Another of the stages is bargaining. A Las Vegas showgirl was admitted to the hospital and it was discovered that she was in the final stages of cancer. A year before she had discovered a lump on her breast, but she chose to ignore the symptoms. Her body was her fortune, and she refused to have it "mutilated," as she described it. When she had to have surgery to save her life she was angry. Soon she thought her beauty was gone, but she still propped herself up in bed and spent hours every day applying makeup. She became garish looking and increasingly bitter. One day a beautiful student nurse came into the room and the show-girl looked at her and remarked to Nurse Nolten, "I would give anything if I could be like…" and then she cut off her bargaining plea and ended pathetically, "But I don't have anything left to give, do I?"

Ironically, at that point she was finally past denying and bargaining and at last able to accept her position. It was then she said, "I can't handle this alone."

When we have "nothing left to give," God says, "All I want is you, beloved. Trust Me." The Great Physician is willing and able to take our burdens, if we will just hand them over to Him. Life and death is not a do-it-yourself project.

DIVINE HEALING: TRUTH AND CONSEQUENCES

When little Erika was on life-support systems, hundreds of people were praying for her healing. Instead, the Lord took Erika to be with Himself. At the same time, in another hospital, Ron Stokes was in intensive care after a severe stroke. Hundreds of people all over the country were praying for Ron. He recovered, and as a result of caring Christian friends, accepted Christ. Why did God cure Ron and not Erika? Were prayers any less fervent or the faith of loved ones any weaker in one case than the other? No, not at all. Does God heal today? Of course He does, but not always. He can heal in response to prayer and faith; He can heal through the skill of physicians or the effectiveness of medicines.

When Ruth's sister, Rosa, was a senior at Wheaton College she collapsed in chapel and was rushed to the hospital. They thought she had appendicitis. Dr. Ken Gieser, who had interned in Dr. Bell's hospital in China, went to the hospital with her. When they operated on Rosa they discovered her abdominal cavity was filled with tubercular nodules. She had to have several months of complete bed rest. The housemother where Ruth and Rosa lived turned over the sunporch to the young patient and Ruth dropped out of school to care for her. She seemed to improve until just before she was to resume normal life when she hemorrhaged from her lungs and they knew she had tuberculosis all through her system. At the small hospital to which she was transferred, the surgeons proposed doing a phrenichotomy on one lung, permanently crushing the phrenic nerve, and a weekly pneumothorax treatment to rest the other.

At that time the Bells returned from China and moved Rosa to a drier climate at a hospital in New Mexico. Ruth stayed with Rosa and watched her attitude with interest. As Ruth said in later years, "There are two kinds of hypocrites in the world, one who wants you to think that they are better than they are and one who wants you to think they are worse than they are. Rosa was one of the latter. She delighted in shocking people. She read her Bible like some people read *Playboy* magazine, shoving it under her pillow when someone came into the room. However, she began to read her Bible in earnest and learned that while Jesus was here on earth, no one came to Him for healing without Jesus healing them. She read where James says, 'Is any one of you sick? He should call the elders of the church to pray over him and anoint him with oil in the name of the Lord. And the prayer offered in faith will make the sick person well...' (James 5:14–15, NIV). Rosa inquired and found a little church that followed those instructions; she called for the elders and they came and prayed for her. Rosa decided she could get up and lead a normal life and stopped the hospital treatments. Medically speaking, she should have hemorrhaged to death."

Ruth remembers her father's reaction to Rosa's decision: "Daddy was concerned. Being a doctor, he knew the dangers involved, but being a man of God he didn't want to discourage Rosa if God was leading her. He talked to the godly superintendent, Mrs. VanDevanter, who ran the hospital, and she said, 'Dr. Bell, there is something special happening in Rosa's life. I would be careful not to discourage it.

"Rosa resumed a normal life, her lungs expanded, and to all

appearances, she was healed. Later, the two doctors who had been treating her in New Mexico, both agnostics, said to Daddy, 'Dr. Bell, your daughter's explanation that God healed her is the only adequate one.'"

Ruth has said that, to her knowledge, from that day until this Rosa has never had a serious illness.

God does heal today and He often spares lives of some who, by human standards, would be dead. Our son, Franklin, has survived many harrowing circumstances, but one is especially vivid to us. This happened while he was a student at the Tourneau College in Texas. He was taking flight instruction and during a spring break his flight instructor and wife, another buddy, and he flew down to Florida to join us for a few days' vacation. When they took off to return it was overcast. As they flew above the clouds, something happened to the electrical system and they lost all the lights on the plane. They descended beneath the cloud cover where they could see the lights of Jackson, Mississippi, and circled until they spotted a small airport. All the lights went on, the strobe lights were flashing, and they made a safe landing.

When the pilot walked over to thank the men in the tower for being so cooperative, they said, "We didn't even know you were coming.... We were just showing some friends around the airport and they wanted to know what would happen if someone came in late at night. We told them we'd turn on the strobe lights, so we demonstrated them. At that moment you came in sight and we couldn't believe it, because we didn't know there was a plane in the area."

God knew Franklin was not ready to go at that time. About two years later his flight instructor was killed in a crash. Sometimes God delivers us from death, and sometimes He doesn't. Only God knows the reason.

Ruth has a friend in England, Jennifer Larcombe, who had developed multiple sclerosis. She prayed for healing, but continued to get worse. She was besieged by people who told her that if everything was right between her and the Lord she would be healed, otherwise she must have some secret sin which she hadn't confessed. This advice was devastating to her, because she loved the Lord with all her heart. Finally, the British publishers, Hodder & Stoughton, asked her to write a book about her experiences. The book was eventually published and was called *Beyond Healing*. Ruth was asked to write the foreword, and when she read the manuscript she was deeply moved. Clearly when God said no to Jennifer, He gave her another ministry.

James said, "And the prayer offered in faith will make the sick person well..." (James 5:15, NIV). And, yet, James himself was beheaded. He trusted God, whatever the outcome.

Soon after James was put to death, Peter was arrested and put in prison. The believers prayed earnestly for Peter, and the night before he was to be brought to trial, an angel rescued him (Acts 12:5–11). In that situation, God said "yes" to Peter.

Christians know that God answers prayer in three ways: yes, no, and later. The apostles of Jesus illustrate this beautifully. After Pentecost, the early church was persecuted severely, but they trusted God in all circumstances. All but one of these apostles died as martyrs, but they were as faithful in their deaths as in their lives, understanding that death is the believer's translation to the presence of the Almighty.

Divine healing or deliverance from death is in His hands.

Sam was a devoted Christian who discovered that he had cancer of the mouth. As the dreadful disease developed, multiple operations took so much of his tongue and face that soon he had very little face left. His wife took him to a healing service and when they returned she told everyone triumphantly that Sam had been healed. It would be impossible to imagine what went on in Sam's mind as his suffering became worse. He hated to have anyone see him, and yet his wife would invite friends and neighbors in and announce that Sam was healed. Instead, he died. In such a case, an unrealistic faith in divine healing can be another form of denial: a belief that comes from disbelief in our own mortality. Christians should have another view of divine healing, and that is to acknowledge God's ability to heal—but to be willing to accept a yes or no answer. Job was God's great example of this belief when he said, "Though he slay me, yet will I hope in him..." (Job 13:15, NIV).

To face the awfulness of disease or illness, knowing that unless God intervenes we will die, is simply being honest. The psalmist says, "The LORD will sustain him on his sickbed and restore him from his bed of illness" (Psalm 41:3, NIV). What a wonderful promise to know that God is with us, caring for us in the room where we are in pain. I have visited Christians in sickrooms where the presence of Christ was so real that, even in the midst of unbelievable suffering and facing death, the patient had serenity.

THE REMARKABLE AMY CARMICHAEL

In 1956 I was in India and visited the Tinnevelly district of South India where Amy Carmichael had lived. Amy was the first missionary to be supported by the Keswich Convention and a woman who wrote forty books during her lifetime. She labored in the land of her adoption for over fifty-six years, never once returning to her home in England on furlough.

I had the honor of visiting the place where she spent the last twenty years of her life, bedridden due to a leg injury from an accident. It was a modest little room, with red tile floor, very few pieces of furniture, and an enormous bird cage outside the window where she could watch the birds.

She had ministered and written from her bed for all those years, and I had a feeling of awe being shown the premises by the woman who had cared for her. As I stood in that simple place, the presence of Christ was very real. Amy went through the valley of the shadow and in spite of pain and physical weakness caused a great light to be spread around the world. It was during those years she did most of her writing—books that still bring blessing to millions around the world. Elisabeth Elliot has written her story in a challenging book entitled *A Chance to Die.*

ALL PRAYERS ANSWERED

Christians in desperate situations search the Scriptures for the many wonderful promises of God. One of our favorites is the statement made by Jesus that "You may ask me for anything in my name, and I will do it" (John 14:14, NIV). We claim that promise and ask the Lord to heal our loved one. But what happens if healing doesn't come? It's easy for Christians to feel guilty or believe our faith is weak if we pray for healing and it doesn't take place. Believers throughout the ages have had to face the fact that God does not heal everyone who prays for healing. But our lack of faith does not determine God's decision on healing. If that were so, He would have to apologize to all of His great servants in the Hebrews 11 Hall of Fame. Look at the cast of characters: Abel, Enoch, Noah, Abraham, Sarah, Isaac, Jacob, Joseph, Moses, Rahab, Gideon, Barak, Samson, Jephtah, David, Samuel, and all the prophets! All of these received great deliverance from God and endured incredible hardships through faith. What happened to them? "Some faced jeers and flogging, while still others were chained and put in prison. They were stoned; they were sawed in two; they were put to death by the sword. They went about in sheepskins and goatskins, destitute, persecuted and mistreated" (Hebrews 11:36–37, NIV).

Even though God was pleased because of their faith, they didn't receive much of the world's pleasures. Why? Because God had a better destination, a heavenly city, waiting for them. It was not because of lack of faith or as a punishment for sin that these men and women of God were not delivered from suffering and death. We have the faith to believe that God has a special glory for those who suffer and die for the sake of Christ.

THE PULPIT ON DEATH ROW

Velma Barfield was a woman from rural North Carolina who was charged with first degree murder; no one could have surmised the effect her life and death would have upon so many people. In 1978 she was arrested for murdering four people, including her mother and fiancé. She never denied her guilt, but told the chilling story of her drug-dazed life, beginning with the tranquilizers which were prescribed following a painful injury.

Velma was a victim of incest as a child and the abuse of prescription drugs as an adult. After she admitted her guilt, she was taken to prison and confined in a cell by herself. One night the guard tuned in to a twenty-four-hour gospel station. Down the gray hall, desperate and alone in her cell, Velma heard the words of an evangelist and allowed Jesus Christ to enter her life. She wrote, "I had been in and out of churches all my life and I could explain all about God. But I had never understood before that Jesus had died for me."

Her conversion was genuine. For six years on death row she ministered to many of her cellmates. The outside world began to hear about Velma Barfield as the story of her remarkable rehabilitation became known. Velma wrote to Ruth and there developed a real friendship between them. In one letter Ruth wrote to Velma, "God has turned your cell on Death Row into a most unusual pulpit. There are people who will listen to what you have to say because of where you are. As long as God has a ministry for you here, He will keep you here. When I compare the dreariness, isolation, and difficulty of your cell to the glory that lies ahead of you, I could wish for your sake that God would say, 'Come on Home.'"5

My daughter, Anne, received special permission to visit Velma Barfield many times and was touched by the sadness of her story and the sincerity of her love for Christ as well as the beauty of her Christian witness in that prison.

Before her final sentence, Velma wrote to Ruth: "If I am executed on August 31, I know the Lord will give me dying grace, just as He gave me saving grace, and has given me living grace." On the night she was executed, Ruth and I knelt and prayed together for her till we knew she was safe in Glory.

Velma Barfield was the first woman in twenty-two years to be executed in the United States. She walked through the valley of the shadow for many years and at her memorial service the Reverend Hugh Hoyle said, "She died with dignity and she died with purpose. Velma is a living demonstration of 'by the grace of God you shall be saved.'"

Ruth wrote the following poem which was read for the benediction at Velma's funeral service:

As the eager parents wait
the homing of their child
from far lands desolate,
from living wild;
wounded and wounding along the way,
their sorrow for sin ignored,
from stain and strain of night and day
to home assured.
So the Heavenly Father waits
the homing of His child;
thrown wide those Heavenly Gates
in welcome glorious-wild,
His, His the joy by right
—once crucified, reviled—
So precious in God's sight
is the death of His child.

WHO CARES?

As Christians we are responsible for one another. "Carry each other's burdens, and in this way you will fulfill the law of Christ.... Therefore, as we have opportunity, let us do good to all people, especially to those who belong to the family of believers"

(Galatians 6:2, 10, NIV). At no time is this more true than when suffering and death touch someone around us.

Often the friends and family who care for a sick loved one touch more lives by their example than they will ever know. But many times we are at a loss to know what to do, or what to say. We stumble in awkward embarrassment, or ignore an unpleasant situation by staying away from someone who is seriously ill. However, members of a family are not meant to suffer alone.

Most of us will have times in our lives when we are with people who are going through the valley of the shadow. How can we show the love of Christ? How would we like others to treat us if we were in similar circumstances? Remember the words of Jesus: "In everything, do to others what you would have them do to you, for this sums up the Law and the Prophets" (Matthew 7:12, NIV).

Margaret Vermeer served as a missionary in Nigeria. When she was seven months pregnant, she received the report that a biopsy of a small tumor was malignant. Five weeks after the surgery to remove the tumor, she gave birth to a son, then began chemotherapy and radiation treatments. For two years she had a miraculous remission, but then gradually more tumors appeared. As her condition grew increasingly serious, she became more sensitive about the way people viewed her. Six months before she died she was speaking for women's church groups, sharing her insights on how to care for others as she wanted to be cared for. Here are some of her thoughts:

First, be honest in sharing your feelings. Don't bounce into the room with false cheerfulness, but admit your helplessness and concern. "I would like to help you, but I don't know how," is a straightforward expression of concern. Don't play games and be evasive. Even children can cope better when people talk to them honestly.

Don't preach a well-thought-out sermon. Christians who bring out their Bibles and read lengthy passages are not being sensitive. To share a verse that means something to you may be helpful, but wait for the signals before plunging into a lengthy spiritual discussion.

Be a good listener. People will tell you what they are ready to talk about. Sickness can be a very lonely journey. When Jesus was agonizing in the Garden of Gethsemane, He didn't want to face death alone. He asked three disciples to wait and pray with Him, but they fell asleep. What good were they?

Treat a dying person as a human being. Sometimes we treat a dying person in such a way that we make it harder on that person emotionally. We shut the people up in hospitals, whisper behind their backs, and deprive them of all the things that had made their lives rich. Familiar things *are* important.

One woman told me that when her mother was in a coma, she put a picture of her father, who had died many years before, on the nightstand beside her mother's bed. Whenever the comatose woman was turned to the other side, she struggled unconsciously to face the photograph of her husband. Finally, her daughter gave instructions to the nurse that whenever her mother was turned she was to move the picture, too. The woman never regained consciousness, but she died with a smile on her face, looking at the picture.

Provide spiritual support. When you quote a Bible verse to comfort a person, be sure you know what the verse means. When Margaret Vermeer knew that she only had a short time to live, she said that she was told by her Christian friends to "give thanks in all circumstances, for this is God's will for you in Christ Jesus" (1 Thessalonians 5:18, NIV). Does that mean to thank God for cancer? Didn't Jesus see sickness and disease as part of Satan's work? Look at the verse carefully. It doesn't say give thanks *for* everything, it says to give thanks *in* everything. There is a vast difference.

When we are told that "God causes everything to work together for good," it doesn't mean that all things are good in themselves, but that God is making them work out for good.

Always have hope. God is greater than the situations we face. Sometimes it's hard to find that which is positive and hopeful, but there is always something to be thankful for. Help the patient look forward to something...a visit from someone special...a time when you will be returning.

My mother loved to anticipate celebrations. A few months before she died, one of her granddaughters was going to be married. Her nurse knew that Mother was too weak to go to the wedding, but she helped her get dressed, anyhow, giving her hope of that occasion. When Mother realized she couldn't go, she was at peace about it. If she had been told from the beginning that she couldn't make it, she would probably have been resentful.

Elisabeth Kübler-Ross made a great contribution to the understanding of death and dying, but her conclusions stand in stark contrast to the hope of the Christian. In an interview she was asked if a patient's religious orientation affected his view toward resignation in the end. She answered, "I have known very few really religious people. The few I have—and I mean those with a deep intrinsic faith—have it much easier, but they are extremely few. Many patients become more religious in the end, but it is not really effective."6

My father-in-law, who had seen many die, said there was a vast difference between the reactions of believers and nonbelievers at the time of death.

In contrast to the anguish and anxiety of the person with no eternal hope, Christians can look to Christ for hope and encouragement. Because of our faith in Christ we do not "...grieve like the rest of men, who have no hope" (1 Thessalonians 4:13b, NIV).

Whatever suffering and agony we must endure, either in our own body or for someone we love, we are assured of His presence. And ultimately we will be resurrected with a body free of pain, an incorruptible and immortal body like His. This is our future hope.

The journey through the valley may be extremely difficult, but what a glorious destination awaits us when we travel with Jesus Christ!

1. Herbert Lockyer, *Last Words of Saints and Sinners* (Grand Rapids, Mich.: Kregel Publications, 1969), 65.

2. *Reader's Digest*, Nov. 1986, 203.

3. Ruth Kopp, *When Someone You Love is Dying* (Grand Rapids, Mich.: Zondervan, 1980), 20.

4. Herbert Lockyer, *All the Promises of the Bible* (Grand Rapids, Mich.: Zondervan, 1962), 200.

5. Velma Barfield, *Women on Death Row,* (Nashville, Tenn.: Oliver Nelson Books, 1985), 141.

6. Elisabeth Kübler-Ross, *Therapeutic Grand Rounds,* No. 36, July 10, 1972.

STRUGGLING

WITH

GOD'S WILL

CHARLES R. SWINDOLL

Charles R. Swindoll, D.D.
President, Dallas Theological Seminary
President, Insight for Living radio ministry
Author of nine Gold Medallion books

"It is a riddle wrapped in a mystery inside an enigma." That is the way the late Sir Winston Churchill once described the actions of Russia. That is also the way many would describe the will of God. As a result, all kinds of approaches and techniques are used to decipher the secret code. Some are so ridiculous they make us shake our heads in disbelief. If they were not employed with such sincerity and devotion, they would be downright hilarious.

SOME UNBELIEVABLE METHODS

If we were looking for a new television series to amuse and entertain, we could name this one "That's Unbelievable!" Here are some examples we could feature on the show.

- A lady received a brochure advertising a tour to Israel. Because going to the Holy Land was one of her lifelong dreams, she really wanted to go. She had the money, the time, the interest, and the strength. But was it God's will? Before going to bed she read the pamphlet once more and noticed that the airplane they would be traveling on was a 747 jumbo jet. After spending a sleepless night wrestling with all the pros and cons, she was greatly relieved the following morning. She now knew it was God's will for her to go. How did she know for sure? When she awoke and glanced at her digital clock, it read 7:47. That was her "sign" from God.

Now, that's unbelievable!

- A collegian needed a car. He didn't know which one God would have him purchase...but as a Christian, he was determined to find God's will before he bought anything. One night he had a series of dreams. Everything in his dreams was yellow. He had his answer. After checking out several used car lots the next day, he finally found the one he was sure the Lord would have him buy. You guessed it. Yellow inside and out. He didn't bother to check it out. He didn't even give it a trial run around the block. It was yellow, so he bought it.

Appropriately, it turned out to be a lemon.

- A pastor had served as a deacon in a church prior to his being called into the ministry. He toyed with the idea of buying a doctor of divinity degree from a degree mill. He really wanted that degree, but he struggled with whether or not it was God's will.

  Late one afternoon he stumbled across the answer he'd been looking for. Because it was in the Bible, all doubt was removed. The Lord had confirmed the minister's desire in 1 Timothy 3:13. The King James Version reads: "For they that have used the office of a deacon well purchase to themselves a good degree."

Now, friends and neighbors, that's unbelievable!

And who hasn't heard about (and tried!) "putting out a fleece" to find God's will?

- Like the woman who had been trying to discover God's will on a particular decision that was almost impossible to determine. Finally she boiled it down to one of two options. Then came the "fleece." As she drove down the street, she told the Lord, "If it is Your will that I choose option A, then keep the light at the next corner green until I get there."
- A similar situation was handled by one man in another manner. His "fleece" was the telephone. He bargained with God, "If it's Your will, then cause my phone to ring at 10:21 tonight."
- I heard recently of a young Christian struggling with the choice of his career. As he was driving and praying in Washington, D.C., he ran out of gas in front of the Philippine Embassy. He got his answer. God wanted him to be a missionary and serve the Lord in the Philippines.

I wonder what this young man would do if he found himself suddenly stuck in an elevator with a young single woman named Mary. Would that be God's "sign" to marry her?

- And who hasn't heard the familiar story of the Christian who sat by a window with the Bible open and allowed the wind to whip the pages over as he picked out a "verse for the day" to claim. His finger fell at random on the words "Judas went and hanged himself." Bewildered and shocked, he tried again and landed on "Go and do thou likewise." Further dismayed he quickly tried a third time as the wind-and-finger method led him to "Whatsoever thou doest, do quickly."

"Ridiculous!" you say. Of course, it is. And so are all these other strange approaches to determining God's will. And yet, we've hardly scratched the surface of the wild and weird methods well-meaning people use to find His will. It happens every day. Among people just like you and me who sincerely want to know the will of God.

SOME GENUINE CONCERNS

Lest we oversimplify the problem, let's understand that there are some legitimate areas of concern that aren't specifically addressed in the Bible. And intelligent, caring, genuine people in God's family are often at a loss to know what He would have them do.

- A high-school senior plays pretty good basketball. He can attend his choice of twelve or fifteen colleges, each offering a full scholarship. Which one is God's will for the Christian athlete?
- A single, happy, well-educated young woman has a good job and a hassle-free life style. But to her surprise she has recently found herself attracted to several young men at her church—all are believers as she is. Should she start thinking seriously about marriage? If so, which one would be God's choice for her?
- A family is living in Southern California. They have numerous friends, a good church, a nice home, and family roots nearby. But mom and dad are starting to hate the smog more and more. The hurried pace mixed with heavy traffic and too many people is starting to take the fun out of life. They want to move—but is it God's will? And if it is, where would He have them live?
- A Christian couple has two children. He wants one or two more. She feels that two are about all she can handle. Both think they know God's will. Which one is right?

And on top of these very real dilemmas, we read in the New Testament: "So then do not be foolish, but understand what the will of the Lord is" (Ephesians 5:17, NASB). Such verses prod us off the fence of indecision, yet we are anxious not to do something "foolish" in the process. Even when our heart is right and our motive is pure, the will of God is not always set forth in a crystal clear manner.

GOD'S DETERMINED WILL

Maybe it will help if we divide the subject into two parts. Think first of God's will as that which He has determined *will* occur. The Bible teaches us that God has a predetermined plan for every life. It is inevitable, unconditional, irresistible, and fixed. It includes and involves everything, such as our circumstances, decisions, achievements, failures, joys and sorrows, sufferings and sins, blessings and calamities, birth and death. Read the following scripture:

> Blessed be the God and Father of our Lord Jesus Christ, who has blessed us with every spiritual blessing in the heavenly places in Christ, just as He chose us in Him before the foundation of the world, that we should be holy and blameless before Him. In love He predestined us to adoption as sons through Jesus Christ to Himself, according to the kind intention of his will, to the praise of the glory of his grace, which He freely bestowed on us in the Beloved. In Him we have redemption through His blood, the forgiveness of our trespasses, according to the riches of His grace, which He lavished upon us. In all wisdom and insight He made known to us the mystery of His will, according to His kind intention which He purposed in Him with a view to an administration suitable to the fulness of the times, that is, the summing up of all things in Christ, things in the heavens and things upon the earth. In Him also we have obtained an inheritance, having been predestined according to His purpose who works all things after the counsel of His will, to the end that we who

were the first to hope in Christ should be to the praise of His glory. In Him, you also, after listening to the message of truth, the gospel of your salvation—having also believed, you were sealed in Him with the Holy Spirit of promise, who is given as a pledge of our inheritance, with a view to the redemption of God's own possession, to the praise of His glory. (Ephesians 1:3–14, NASB)

That says at length what Daniel 4:35 says in brief:

"And all the inhabitants of the earth are accounted as nothing. But He does according to His will in the host of heaven and among the inhabitants of earth; and no one can ward off His hand or say to Him, "What has Thou done?"

God, our sovereign and immutable Master, openly declares that life is no will o' the wisp encounter with luck. His determined will is being accomplished free of frustration. The plan is comprehensive in scope and complete down to the tiniest detail. And it is all for His glory. Rather than causing us to fear, the truth is designed to put us at ease and calm our anxieties.

But what about sin? Was sin a part of God's determined will? Yes, it was. It neither shocked nor frustrated our eternal God when sin occurred in the Garden of Eden. His eternal plan included the sacrificial death of His Son for sinful man. Read for yourself 1 Peter 1:18–21; Acts 2:23; Luke 22:22. Christ's payment for our sin was no divine afterthought.

But doesn't this make God responsible for sin? No, in no way. Let no one say when he is tempted, "I am being tempted by God"; for God cannot be tempted by evil, and He Himself does not tempt any one. But each one is tempted when he is carried away and enticed by his own lust. Then when lust has conceived, it gives birth to sin; and when sin is accomplished, it brings forth death. (James 1:13–15, NASB)

The Scripture never points a finger of blame at God regarding sin. When we humans commit sin, it is a human responsibility.

"O Jerusalem, Jerusalem, who kills the prophets and stones those who are sent to her! How often I wanted to gather your children together, the way a hen gathers her chicks under her wings, and you were unwilling." (Matthew 23:37, NASB)

GOD'S DESIRED WILL

That verse helps us see that there is another side of the coin. The Lord Jesus Christ declared with a heavy heart that he often wanted to gather the citizens of Jerusalem around Him, but they resisted and refused. His "desire" was to meet with them and have them respond positively to His offer of love, but they were "unwilling."

Back again into Ephesians 5, we are told not to be unwise (5:15). That's God's desired will for us. But how often we resist His desire! We are told not to be foolish (5:17) or to get drunk (5:18). That is His desire, but it isn't always what happens. He tells husbands to love their wives (5:25). But the decision to obey is the husband's to make. You see, God's desired will calls for a human response...which leaves room for His desire not to be fulfilled. A simple chart will help:

DETERMINED WILL	DESIRED WILL
Predestined	Calls for our cooperation
Comprehensive, eternal	Limited, temporal
It will occur	It may or may not occur
Cannot be frustrated	It can be resisted
Emphasis: God's sovereignty	Emphasis: Man's responsibility
Purpose: To glorify God	Purpose: To glorify God

Some of my ultra-Calvinistic friends who struggle as they read this will say, "But haven't you read Psalm 32:8?"

I will instruct you and teach you in the way which you should go: I will counsel you with My eye upon you.

"Clearly, God takes full responsibility," they assert. "He promises to instruct, to teach, to lead us in the way...and that means it is *all* up to Him!" they add. Yes, I have read that verse, but I have also read the verse that follows, which warns me, "Do not be as the horse or as the mule...." You see, His desire for us to obey His leading can be blocked if we fail to cooperate like a self-willed horse or a stubborn mule.

Many who discover these two sides to the will of God often want to know if it is possible for us to know His determined will. My friend, author J. Grant Howard, answers that quite well.

Can I know the determined will of God for my life? Yes—after it has occurred!

You now know that God's determined will for your life was that you be born of certain parents, in a certain location, under certain conditions, and that you be male or female. You now know that God determined for you to have certain features, certain experiences, certain teachers, certain interests, certain friends, a certain kind of education, and certain brothers and/or sisters, or perhaps to be an only child. In other words, everything that has happened in your life to this moment has been part of God's determined will for your life. It has happened because He has determined it to be so.

What about the future? Can I know any part of God's determined will for my life in the future? Your spiritual position and eternal destiny are the only two things you can know with certainty. If you are in Christ now, you can know for certain that you will remain in Christ at every moment in the future (John 5:24; 10:27–29; Romans 5:1; 2 Corinthians 5:17). If you are not a Christian, you are in sin right now and you can know for certain that you will remain in that spiritually dead position in the future unless and until you personally receive Christ as your Savior (Ephesians 2:1–3)....

The remainder of your future is hidden from you until it happens. Your career, marriage partner, home location, grades in school, friends, sicknesses, accidents, honors, travels, income, retirement, etc., are all part of God's determined will but are not revealed to you ahead of time....

What should be the Christian's attitude toward the determined will of God? He should recognize it as a reality— clearly taught in the Word of God. Rest in it as good, because that's what God says about it—He causes all things to work together for good to those who love Him (Romans 8:28). Beyond that, don't worry about it and don't try to figure it out, because His ways are unfathomable (Romans 11:33).[1]

Having come to terms with this clarification, we are now able to pursue the solution to two crucial issues: How does God make His will known? And how can I know if I am in His will?

HOW DOES GOD MAKE HIS WILL KNOWN?

I cannot get into all phases of the subject, so I must assume several things.

1. I'll assume that you are fairly healthy, physically and emotionally. If not, it is doubtful that you can correctly follow the guidelines I'm going to suggest with the level of sensitivity needed for such a pursuit. Poor health tends to create a mental or emotional fog in the process of interpreting God's will.

2. I'll assume you really *want* to know His will. Unless this is true, numerous problems are created that again block a proper flow of understanding.

3. I'll assume you are willing to adapt, change, and flex if you discover such is needed. Obedience is essential. Doing God's will is the flip side of discovering it.

4. I'll assume you are a Christian—one who knows God personally through faith in His Son. This is "family truth" that can be applied by family members only.

Now then, let me ask you to stop, look, and listen. God makes His desires known to those who stop at His Word, look in with a sensitive spirit, and listen to others. When we go to His Word, we stop long enough to hear from above. When we look, we examine our surrounding circumstances in light of what He is saying to our inner spirit (perhaps you prefer to call this your conscience). And when we listen to others, we seek the counsel of wise, qualified people.

Stop at the Scriptures

The Bible tells us that the entrance of God's Word gives light (Psalm 119:130), that it is a lamp for our feet and a light that shines brightly on our path (Psalm 119:105). God has placed His Word in our hands and allowed it to be translated into our tongue (both were His *determined* will) so we could have a much more objective set of guidelines to follow than dreams, digital clock readings, hunches, impulses, and feelings. Sixty-six books filled with precepts and principles. And the better we know His Word, the more clearly we will know His will.

Precepts. Some of the statements that appear in the Bible are specific, black-and-white truths that take all the guesswork out of the way. Here are a few:

For this is the will of God, your sanctification; that is, that you abstain from sexual immorality....(1 Thessalonians 4:3, NASB)

Sexual immorality is never the will of God. Never!

See that no one repays another with evil for evil, but always seek after that which is good for one another and for all men. Rejoice always; pray without ceasing; in everything give thanks; for this is God's will for you in Christ Jesus. (1 Thessalonians 5:15–18, NASB)

These specific things are stated to be the will of God. There are even times that suffering is directly the will of God for us. First Corinthians 7 says a lot about remaining single as well as being committed to one's marriage. Clearly, this chapter (along with 2 Corinthians 6:14) states that a Christian is definitely not to marry a non-Christian. These are finely tuned precepts that reveal God's will.

Principles. But the Bible also has principles...general guidelines to assist us through the gray areas. Not so much "do this" and "don't do that," but an appeal to use wisdom and discretion when such are needed.

We have both precepts and principles in our traffic laws. The sign that reads "Speed Limit 35" is a precept. The one that reads "Drive Carefully" is a principle. And that principle will mean one thing on a deserted street at two o'clock in the morning...but something else entirely at three-thirty in the afternoon when children are walking home from school.

Just remember this: A primary purpose of the Word of God is to help us know the will of God. Become a careful, diligent student of Scripture. Those who are will be better equipped to understand His desires and walk in them.

Look Around and Within

Philippians 2:12–13 presents a good cause for our cooperating with the Lord's leading.

> So then, my beloved, just as you have always obeyed, not as in my presence only, but now much more in my absence, work out your salvation with fear and trembling; for it is God who is at work in you, both to will and to work for His good pleasure.

These verses highlight three specifics: There's a willingness to obey. There's the need to "work out" or give ourselves to doing our part with a sensitive spirit (fear and trembling). And then there's the promise that God will "work in you" to pull off His plan. As we remain alert to His working, paying close attention to doors He opens and closes, He directs us into His will.

This reminds me of Paul on the second missionary journey. He crossed the vast country we know today as Turkey, hoping and trying to preach the gospel...but one door after another slammed in his face (read Acts 16:6–10). Finally, on the western-most edge of the country, at the town named Troas, God announced to him that He wanted Paul to go further west into Europe and proclaim the truth over there. An open door awaited him.

Closed doors are just as much God's leading as open ones. The believer who wants to do God's will *must* remain sensitive and cooperative, not forcing his way into areas that God closes off. The Lord uses circumstances and expects us to "read" them with a sensitive, alert conscience.

We *must* stop and check His Word. We *must* look around and within. And there is one more helpful piece of advice to remember. We *must*...

Listen to the Counsel of Qualified People

Solomon the wise once wrote:

A plan in the heart of a man is like deep water, but a man of understanding draws it out. (Proverbs 20:5, NASB)
Iron sharpens iron, so one man sharpens another. As in water face reflects face, so the heart of man reflects man. (Proverbs 27:17, 19, NASB)

Jethro, Moses' father-in-law, gave him good counsel when he challenged him to delegate his work load (Exodus 18). Older women in God's family are told to instruct and encourage the younger women (Titus 2:3–5). Colossians 3:16 and Romans 15:14 exhort Christians to counsel and admonish each other. It is a great help to have the wise, seasoned, objective insights of those who are mature in the faith.

Like a quarterback, facing fourth-and-one on the thirty-yard line, who calls a time-out to consult with the coach, so must we. God uses others to help us know His desires.

God makes His will known: (1) through His Word...as we stop and study it, (2) through circumstances...as we look within and sense what He is saying, and (3) through the counsel of others...as we listen carefully.

HOW CAN I KNOW I AM IN GOD'S WILL?

God *wants* us to know and do His will. He consistently and diligently works on our behalf to assure us and affirm us. He gives us two specific "green light" signals within to help us know we are fulfilling his desires.

Peace

And let the peace of Christ rule in your hearts, to which indeed you were called in one body; and be thankful. (Colossians 3:15, NASB)

Peace "acts as umpire" (literally) within us. We become increasingly more assured deep down inside. In the words of Romans 14:5, we become "fully convinced" in our own minds.

Satisfaction

In addition to peace, there is this abiding pleasure and satisfaction. We love doing it. Lots of internal itches are scratched. This explains why some who could make much more money in another profession stay in the ranks of teaching. And why some endure the pressure of a certain calling year after year without seriously considering a change to something easier.

Sir Flinders Petrie, the father of Palestinian archaeology, once wrote a friend who questioned his motive for doing what he was doing. Part of the letter aptly illustrates the level of satisfaction God can give:

> "You seem to take for granted that as I am not working for money... I must therefore be working for fame,..." he said. "But would you be surprised to hear that this is not my mainspring? I work because I can do what I am doing, better than I can do anything else.... And I am aware that such work is what I am best fitted for. If credit of any sort comes from such work, I have no objection of any sort to it; but it is not what stirs me to work at all. I believe that I should do just the same in quantity and quality if all that I did was published in someone else's name."[2]

SOME OFTEN ASKED QUESTIONS

There are several questions that people often ask regarding God's will. Let's consider four of the more common ones.

1. What if I know the will of God but deliberately do not do it?
Unhappily, this does occur. Imperfect human beings are, at times, openly disobedient. What happens on those occasions? As in every area of life, when we don't play by the rules, we must pay the consequences. But consequences don't usually happen immediately. In fact, for a temporary period of time things may run along smoothly. Hebrews 11:25 mentions enjoying the passing pleasure of sin. Sin offers its pleasures...but they are short-lived.

Remember Jonah? He was able to buy a ticket on the ship leaving for Tarshish and he was even able to fall asleep. But by and by, he found himself in a threatening storm and finally in the belly of the fish. God brings discipline upon His children. This includes external consequences as well as internal conflicts. Guilt and heartache rage within. If you question that, check out David's words in Psalm 32:3–4. After his disobedience connected with the Bathsheba affair, the man admits maximum misery within.

On top of all this there can be public embarrassment and shame as fellow Christians in the body of Christ are impacted. When necessary discipline must be administered by the church (Matthew 18:15–17), the disobedience you tried to keep secret becomes public knowledge. Your family also suffers. We are not isolated individuals. Like dominoes standing on end, when one falls others are affected.

2. Can't I rely on my feelings? This is frequently asked with regard to things we really want to do...but for which we lack biblical support. Take the case of a young woman madly in love with the man of her dreams. She is a Christian, but he is not. But, of course, he promises her he will be "everything a husband ought to be." And he will not interfere with her interests in the Lord. She can trust him to give her plenty of space to attend church, have Christian friends—whatever. She just *knows* he is the one! And she believes with all her heart he will someday change. He will become a Christian, she is confident, after they get married. How does she think it's God will? Her feelings. He makes her *feel* so good. He's the kind of a man she's always wanted.

But the Bible states unequivocally that to be unequally yoked with an unbeliever is *not* God's will, her feelings notwithstanding. Second Corinthians 6:14–18 and 1 Corinthians 7:39 are not eased by warm feelings and romantic moonlit nights. No matter how strong our feelings may be, when there are biblical precepts and/or principles that point us in a certain direction, we dare not ignore or disobey God's Word.

3. Can I be in the will of God and not know it? Yes, indeed. In fact, I'm of the opinion many Christians are! While it is true that God desires us to be "filled with the knowledge of His will" (Colossians 1:9, NASB), many believers are not at that level of awareness. Furthermore, there is the weird yet popular idea that God's will is always something uncomfortable, painful, or unfulfilling. To some, it is inconceivable that God's will could be enjoyable and even delightful. Romans 12:2 states very clearly that His will is "...good, acceptable, and perfect." Yes, we can say and do certain things that are in harmony with God's will and yet not be aware of it.

Quite honestly, we can cultivate certain habits that are pleasing to Him and consistently carry them out without even thinking about their being His will. This would include things like cultivating good personal relationships, keeping short accounts with sin, paying our bills promptly, maintaining a healthy body through a nutritius diet and sufficient exercise, and reacting correctly to stress.

4. What about specifics that aren't addressed in Scripture? The Bible doesn't tell the Christian specifically where to live. Or which career to pursue. Or where to go to college. If it did, how easy it would be...yet how little faith we would need! That would reduce the Bible to a vocational guidance handbook, nothing more than a divinely inspired telephone directory...and just about as interesting. Our spiritual maturity would be no deeper than a third-grader.

As I mentioned earlier, God gives us principles. He also moves and works through circumstances. He even "speaks" to us through the wise counsel of a friend. All of this keeps us trusting, depending, waiting, praying, reading His Word, and using healthy doses of common sense.

The emphasis in Scripture is on who a person is and what a person does rather than on where a person lives. I have a family in mind who recently moved from Southern California to Washington. Some very close friends of theirs really wanted to move with them...but they had no leading from God that it was His will. Couple "A" has a child whose health is endangered by living in this area. As loving parents responding to the needs of their child, they packed up and left. Couple "B" has three children—healthy and happy—and are deeply involved in a discipleship ministry. For them to leave right now (even though they genuinely *want* to) would not be God's will. They have no peace in their hearts when they think seriously about joining their friends in Washington.

If the Lord wants you to get a specific message and to respond in an explicit manner, He has dozens of ways to communicate that to you. No mumbo-jumbo, no sky writing, no magic tricks or middle-of-the-night voices need to be sought. Those who really want to do His will, will know it (John 7:17).

Let me add this final piece of advice I often employ. When someone is convinced that God is leading him in a specific direction and you are not so convinced—yet you haven't a particular precept or principle from the Bible to point out why you disagree—learn a lesson from Paul's friends in Acts 21. The apostle was absolutely determined to go to Jerusalem, even though he knew danger lurked at every turn. Equally convinced to the contrary, a group of Christian friends (including his physician companion Dr. Luke) attempted to change his plans. Unsuccessful, they backed off out of respect. Verse 14 says it all:

And since he would not be persuaded, we fell silent, remarking, "The will of the Lord be done!"

Each believer is independently accountable to God for his/her response to the Lord's specific leading, even though others don't understand or agree.

THE MOST SATISFYING EXPERIENCE IN LIFE

No, finding God's will is not magical or mysterious. He hasn't hidden it in a digital clock or wrapped it in a complex riddle that calls for open windows or dreams and traffic lights to solve. He has given us all we need to know it...His Book, daily circumstances, an inner spirit, and some wise friends. As I stated earlier, I'm convinced many are in His will who think they are not, because they are so fulfilled and happy in life. Surprising to some, God's will is the most satisfying experience in all of life.

Oh, by the way...for you who are not Christians, you'd be interested to know that God has a desire for you, too. It is spelled out in simple terms in a verse in the Bible. Patiently God awaits your coming to Him.

> ...not wishing for any to perish, but for all to come to repentance. (2 Peter 3:9, NASB)

Replace the word "any" with *your* name, my friend. It is His desire for you to change your mind concerning His Son, Jesus Christ. If you will, He will give you His life and His forgiveness. But if you won't, you will perish. Please, do not delay. Please accept His offer right now.

Dear Father:

I am grateful for the clear, unmistakable way Your Word communicates Your truth. Your will is not something to fear, but rather to accept and enjoy...because it is for our good and Your glory.

Thank you for pushing back the fog of misunderstanding so that we can see and grasp the significance of this all-important subject. Tenderly yet firmly, work with us so that we don't drift from the nucleus of Your will, which is really the safest place to be on the face of this earth.

In the matchless name of Your son. Amen.

1. J. Howard, Jr., *Knowing God's Will—and Doing It!* (Grand Rapids, Mich.: Zondervan Publishing House, 1976), 14–16.

2. Joseph A. Calloway, *"Sir Flinders Petrie, Father of Palestinian Archaeology,"* Biblical Archaeology Review, 6 (November/December 1980), 51.

NOTES

"Struggling with Guilt and Bitterness" taken from *He Still Moves Stones* by Max Lucado, © 1993 by Max Lucado. Used by permission of Word Publishing, Nashville, Tennessee. All rights reserved.

"Struggling with Forgiveness" originally published as *Experiencing God's Forgiveness* by Luis Palau, © 1984 by Luis Palau. Published by Multnomah Press. Used by permission of the author. All rights reserved.

"Struggling with Moral Purity" originally published as *Moral Purity* by Charles R. Swindoll, © 1985, 1986 by Charles R. Swindoll. Published by Insight for Living. Used by permission of the author. All rights reserved.

"Struggling with Marriage" originally published as "Commitment," taken from *Marriage: Experiencing the Best* by Steve Stephens, © 1995 by Steve Stephens. Published by Vision House Publishing, Inc. Used by permission of the author. All rights reserved.

"Struggling with Parenting" originally published as "The Three Chairs" and "Raising Godly Children," taken from *First Hand Faith* by Bruce H. Wilkinson, © 1996 by Bruce Wilkinson and Chip MacGregor. Used by permission of Multnomah Publishers, Inc. All rights reserved.

"Struggling with Money" originally published as "Money: The Currency of Christian Hedonism," taken from *Desiring God* by John Piper, © 1996 by John Piper. Used by permission of Multnomah Publishers, Inc. All rights reserved.

"Struggling with Depression" originally published as *Getting through Depression* by Charles M. Sell, © 1984 by Charles M. Sell. Published by Multnomah Press. Used by permission of the author. All rights reserved.

"Struggling with Self-Image" originally published as "Why